The Battle
for Burma

The Battle for Burma

An Illustrated History

Roy Conyers Nesbit

Pen & Sword
MILITARY

First published in Great Britain in 2009 by
Pen & Sword Military
an imprint of
Pen & Sword Books Ltd
47 Church Street
Barnsley
South Yorkshire
S70 2AS

ISBN 978 1 84415 955 0

Typeset in Palatino by
Phoenix Typesetting, Auldgirth, Dumfriesshire

Printed and bound in England by
CPI UK

Pen & Sword Books Ltd incorporates the Imprints of Pen & Sword Aviation, Pen & Sword
Maritime, Pen & Sword Military, Wharncliffe Local History, Pen and Sword Select,
Pen and Sword Military Classics and Leo Cooper.

For a complete list of Pen & Sword titles please contact
PEN & SWORD BOOKS LIMITED
47 Church Street, Barnsley, South Yorkshire, S70 2AS, England
E-mail: enquiries@pen-and-sword.co.uk
Website: www.pen-and-sword.co.uk

Contents

Acknowledgements

My thanks are due to those who have provided research into this book, as well as those who have provided photographs. They are Squadron Leader J.D. Braithwaite; the late J.M. Bruce; Wing Commander C.J. Craig; Chris Davies; Alan Fox DFM; F.W. Guy; Rupert Harding; Roger Hayward; G.S. Leslie; Glyn Loosmore MM, CdeG; The Medmenham Club; Jim Muncie; my brother Michael H. Nesbit; Air Commodore Graham R. Pitchfork MBE; the late Wing Commander F.D. Proctor; Squadron Leader T.N. Rosser; Roger Trayhurn of Swindon Central Library; the late Group Captain S.G. Wise; Gerrit J. Zwanenburg MBE, KON.

Special thanks must go to my friend Squadron Leader Dudley Cowderoy and his wife Jane (née Kirk) for their patience in checking the narrative and captions of photographs, as well as making suggestions for improvement.

The Publishers have included several historically important wartime photographs that cannot be reproduced to our usual high standards. It was felt that they were of sufficient interest to the reader to be included.

CHAPTER ONE

A String of Disasters

Britain's war with Japan had its origins in the abrogation in 1922 of the Anglo-Japanese Alliance. The two countries had been on friendly terms since 1906, when the first of these treaties had been signed. This had been at a time when Japan was emerging from centuries of feudal isolation and beginning to develop industries with the aid of Western technology. Indeed, Japan had entered the First World War in support of Britain and France by protecting their interests in the Pacific and China. In those days, the British public regarded the Japanese as akin to themselves in some respects, people of a group of islands roughly the same size as the British Isles.

However, Britain became weakened after the First World War, with the loss of a million servicemen as well as most of her gold reserves. Disarmament was the policy favoured by her people, and the country was no longer able to provide adequate military support for her Commonwealth and Empire. Increased dependence on America for naval strength in the Pacific became essential. On 6 February 1922 a treaty was signed in Washington by America, the British Commonwealth, France, Italy and Japan. This sought to regulate the various naval strengths in the Pacific and it was followed by two other treaties which attempted to guarantee the integrity of China.

These treaties soon began to thwart the Japanese desire for expansion, for her population had grown apace until by 1925 it had almost doubled to 60 million since 1880. With few natural resources, Japan looked to interests in China and elsewhere in the Pacific for sustenance and development. Moreover, the accession of Emperor Hirohito to the throne in 1926 ushered in a period of intense nationalism coupled with increasing military strength. The Japanese invasion of Manchuria in 1931 and subsequent advances into China were followed by links with Nazi Germany and Fascist Italy when she signed the Anti-Comintern Pact in 1936, opposing the Soviet Union.

The growing military strength and industrial prowess within Japan began to alarm other countries with interests in the Far East, particularly the USA, Britain, Australia, New Zealand and the Netherlands. Rearmament against new dictatorships began in Britain but it was too little and too late, as well as concentrated on the threat from continental Europe. Each of the three services clamoured for resources, but the main increase in production centred on the RAF. No battle fleet was available for the Far East, where it was hoped that any conflict would be less likely.

Of course, concern about the situation in the Far East intensified after the German Blitzkrieg in Western Europe during the spring of 1940 and the fall of France, with the partition of that country into German-occupied and Vichy France. French possessions in Indo-China and Cambodia came under the control of the latter, and Japan began to take advantage of this weakness. Her troops moved into the northern area of Indo-China on 23 September 1940 and soon gained control of the entire country, as well as Cambodia.

These occupations posed an immediate threat to Malaya, part of the British Commonwealth, for the Japanese looked longingly at the country's rich deposits of tin and oil as well as her huge rubber plantations, and ultimately at the great naval base of Singapore. America had imposed sanctions on Japan, cutting off most imports of these vital products. However, accurate intelligence in Britain about Japanese intentions was not forthcoming. The Government Code and Cipher School at Bletchley Park had managed to break the Japanese naval code and was able to keep track of movements of warships, but these decrypts did not disclose any forthcoming operations with certainty.

The British Government hoped that a force of American, British and Dutch military units could be formed under a single command for defensive purposes in the Pacific. But America was unwilling to participate in such an arrangement. Her policy was that of isolation, bent on protecting her western seaboard and the Pacific islands which came under her control. President Franklin D. Roosevelt was reluctant to take measures that appeared to sustain British colonial requirements. The Netherlands had been occupied by the Wehrmacht, while its possessions in the East Indies had only meagre forces for their protection.

Thus Britain was forced to rely on her own resources for the defence of Malaya, but these were extremely limited. Much of her modern military equipment had been lost in the retreat of the British Expeditionary Force from France and the evacuation via Dunkirk. That which remained was vital for the defence of the home country. The French Navy was no longer available for defence against Italy in the Mediterranean, and the Royal Navy was committed to that area as well as to the defence of Britain and her sea lanes. The RAF had suffered severe losses in France and was building up for the conflict which became known as the Battle of Britain.

Within Malaya and Singapore overall defence came under Air Chief Marshal Sir Robert Brooke-Popham, who had been appointed as Commander-in-Chief Far East on 12 October 1941. Vice-Admiral Sir Geoffrey Layton commanded the Eastern Fleet but the warships at his disposal were quite inadequate. By December 1941 those available for combat consisted of three six-inch cruisers, one destroyer, seven gunboats, two armed merchant cruisers and eight motor torpedo-boats. However, on 2 December 1941 the battleship HMS *Prince of Wales* and the battle cruiser HMS *Repulse* arrived at Singapore, together with three destroyers. They

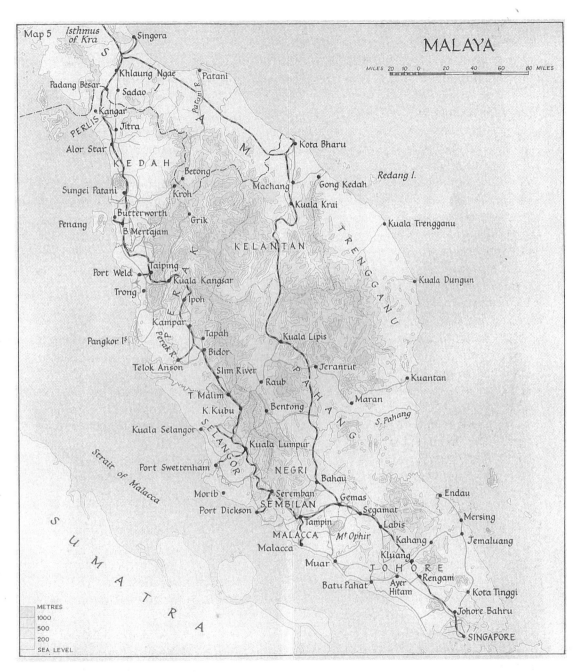

Malaya and Singapore in 1941/2.

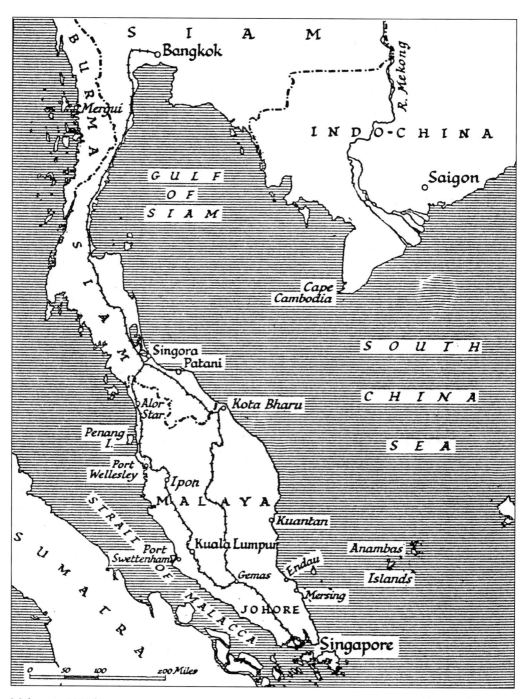

Malaya in 1941/2.

were under the command of Admiral Sir Tom Phillips and had been dispatched on the insistence of Winston Churchill, who hoped that their presence would act as a deterrent to any Japanese thoughts of invasion. Meanwhile the Admiralty decided that they were having no deterrent effect and that they would be in danger from Japanese submarines. Phillips was advised to move eastwards and on 5 December *Repulse* and the destroyers set off for Darwin in Australia, while *Prince of Wales* remained in dry dock for the removal of barnacles.

Lieutenant-General A.E. Percival was the General Officer Commanding Malaya, and his forces seemed quite formidable in numerical terms. Singapore was manned by two infantry brigades plus coastal and anti-aircraft defences. Malaya was defended by the 12th Indian Infantry Brigade, III Indian Corps with its 9th and 11th Divisions, and the 8th Australian Division. In total these forces seemed very strong but they were not sufficiently mechanised or equipped with modern weapons, and were inadequately trained. Local Volunteer Groups had been formed from the civil population, but these had received few weapons and only scant training.

Much reliance was placed on the RAF, commanded by Air Vice-Marshal C.M. Pulford, but the total squadron strength in early December 1941 consisted merely of forty-seven Bristol Blenheims, sixty Brewster Buffalos, twenty-four Vickers Vildebeests, twenty-four Lockheed Hudsons and three Consolidated Catalina flying boats. These totalled 158 aircraft, of which the Vildebeests were obsolescent. It was estimated that this number formed only a third of the minimum strength needed for the defence of Malaya and Singapore, even with the prevalent but mistaken belief that Japanese aircraft and pilots were inferior to their Western counterparts.

On 6 December 1941 three Hudsons of 1 (RAAF) Squadron were on reconnaissance sorties from their airfield at Kota Bharu in north-east Malaya when two of them reported a large Japanese convoy off the south-east tip of Indo-China, heading westwards towards the Gulf of Siam. 'No. 1 Degree of Readiness' was announced in Singapore and HMS *Renown* and the destroyers were immediately recalled. A Catalina of 205 Squadron was dispatched from the island, but the message it carried was never received for it was shot down by a Nakajima Ki-27 fighter. Other attempts at air reconnaissance during the following day were hampered by bad weather.

The Japanese convoy consisted of eighteen large transports from the island of Hainan, which were joined by seven more from Saigon. It was carrying 26,500 highly trained assault troops of the 5th Infantry Division and the 56th Infantry Regiment, the vanguard of the Japanese 25th Army commanded by General Tomoyuki Yamashita. It was also carrying the 55th Division of the 15th Army commanded by Lieutenant-General Shojiro Iida.

Close escort for the convoy was provided by a battleship, six cruisers and thirteen destroyers. Seaplane tenders and some of the warships carried reconnaissance floatplanes, the Aichi E13A 'Jake' and the Mitsubishi F1M 'Pete', but the main air cover was provided by squadrons of land-based aircraft from airfields near Saigon and on the island of Phuquoc off the south-west of Indo-China. These squadrons were equipped in total with about 300 aircraft, most of them modern. Among them were the Nakajima fighters Ki-27 'Kate' and Ki-43 'Oscar', as well as the Mitsubishi fighters A5M 'Claude' and A6M 'Zero'. Others were equipped with long-range bombers, the Mitsubishi G3M 'Nell' and the G4M 'Betty'. There were also a few reconnaissance aircraft. The English names for Japanese aircraft were given to them by the Allies, as a simple means of recognition.

At 0905 hours on the following day the Japanese convoy reached a central point in the Gulf of Siam and the transports split up and began heading for different objectives. Those carrying troops of the 15th Army headed for Siamese ports in the northern sector of the Kra Isthmus. Some carrying the 25th Army headed for the Siamese ports of Singora and Patani near the northern border of Malaya, while three headed directly for the Malayan port of Kota Bharu, close to Siam.

Events on 8 December 1941 marked the beginning of the war between Japan and the Western Allies. The first indication at Singapore took place at about 0400 hours after radar picked up the approach of some seventeen hostile aircraft. These were G3M 'Nell' long-range bombers, the only aircraft from a larger force that had managed to get through bad weather after taking off from Indo-China. They targeted the docks and airfields but some of the bombs fell in civilian quarters, causing deaths and injuries. Singapore was also rife with rumours of a Japanese air attack on the US Navy at Pearl Harbor in Hawaii. Details were not known at the time, but all eight battleships of the US Pacific Fleet had been sunk or put out of action, together with three cruisers, three destroyers and several auxiliary aircraft. The attackers had also destroyed 188 aircraft for the loss of only 29 of their own number. It was a stunning victory for the carrier-borne Japanese Naval Air Force.

The war began soon after midnight at Kota Bharu in Malaya, when Japanese troops from the 5th Division began disembarking from landing craft at the mouth of a river. There was also a bombardment from a Japanese cruiser and three destroyers which had accompanied the three transports. No. 1 (RAAF) Squadron was alerted and its Hudsons began a series of sorties against vessels which could be seen clearly in the darkness. They strafed and bombed the landing craft and transports for several hours, returning several times to re-arm. Many barges were sunk and two of the transports were damaged so badly that they had to withdraw, but some of the Hudsons were shot down or returned damaged. The Japanese suffered severe casualties but many assault troops stormed ashore and drove back the defending troops of 9th Indian Division, part of III Indian Corps, after fierce fighting and heavy losses on both sides. The defending troops began to withdraw southwards down the difficult road towards Kuala Lipis in central Malaya.

Meanwhile, aircraft from other airfields were ordered to give support to 1

(RAAF) Squadron. Vildebeests of 36 Squadron from Gong Kedah made torpedo attacks on the cruiser but scored no hits. Hudsons of 8 (RAAF) Squadron and Blenheims of 60 Squadron based at Kuantan, situated further south, did not arrive quickly enough. Blenheims of 62 Squadron at Alor Star, off the north-west coast of Malaya, took off to bomb the Japanese assault troops at Patani in Siam, but found no targets. However, a lone Bristol Beaufort II of 100 Squadron, which had previously arrived at Kota Bharu from Singapore, took off on a reconnaissance sortie over Patani. It was attacked by A6M 'Zeros' and seriously damaged, but the pilot escaped in cloud and managed to return with photographs confirming the Japanese landings. The invaders had met some resistance from Siamese troops but they soon succeeded in capturing the airfields.

So far, the RAF and the RAAF in northern Malaya had lost nine aircraft in these activities but they were allowed no respite. From 0700 hours onwards their airfields were attacked remorselessly by over a hundred Japanese long-range fighters and bombers operating from Indo-China. By the end of the day more than fifty aircraft had been destroyed or seriously damaged on the ground. The

Bristol Beaufort II serial T9543 of 100 Squadron photographed at RAF Seletar in Singapore on 5 December 1941. It was flown by Flight Lieutenant P.D.F. Mitchell from RAF Kota Bharu on 8 December to photograph the Japanese landings in the Singora area and returned successfully, despite being damaged by Japanese fighters. Later on the same day it was destroyed by a Japanese strafing attack on the airfield.

Author's collection

number available for operations in northern Malaya was halved during this black day. However, there was some welcome reinforcement during the day when three squadrons of the Royal Netherlands Air Force arrived at Singapore with nine Buffalo fighters and twenty-two Martin 139W bombers. Assistance was certainly needed as Japanese fighters began to stream down from Indo-China to operate from the airfields captured in southern Siam, and threatened to dominate the skies over Malaya.

Another major calamity began on the same day. Admiral Tom Phillips could not bear the thought of the forces in north Malaya resisting Japanese attacks without help from the Royal Navy. In the early evening *Prince of Wales* and *Repulse* slipped out of Singapore with four destroyers and then headed north, with the objective of cutting off and destroying the invasion fleet. Phillips hoped for reconnaissance and fighter escort from the RAF and was not aware of the threat from Japanese torpedo-bombers.

Low cloud obscured the British fleet, known as Force Z, during the beginning of its passage but it was spotted by a Japanese submarine at 1400 hours on the next day, 9 December. Japanese reconnaissance aircraft flew over the fleet at 1835 hours but Phillips stayed on course. Then he received a signal stating that what seemed to be a Japanese transport was approaching Kuantan. This later proved to be mistaken but Phillips altered course south-west towards the coast.

Meanwhile a huge attack force of eighty-seven Japanese bombers had been organised from the airfields near Saigon, consisting of G3M 'Nells' and G4M 'Betties'. Of these, twenty-five were armed with bombs while the others carried torpedoes. They found Force Z soon after midday on 10 December, steaming without escort by RAF fighters although Buffalos of 453 (RAAF) Squadron were en route. All the Japanese aircraft went into the attack. The warships responded with curtains of anti-aircraft fire and attempted to 'comb the tracks' of torpedoes, but eventually both major vessels succumbed. It was estimated that six torpedoes and several bombs hit *Prince of Wales*, and she sank at 1222 hours. Bombs as well as five torpedoes hit *Repulse*, which heeled over and sank at 1233 hours.

The destroyers picked up 2,081 men from the two warships, including Captain W.G. Tennant, the captain of *Repulse*. Admiral Tom Phillips and Captain J.C. Leach of *Prince of Wales* were among a total of 840 men who did not survive the sinkings. Just two Japanese aircraft had been shot down, although many others were damaged, one so badly that it crashed on return.

This air-sea battle resulted in a stupendous victory for the Japanese. Within little more than two days they had gained command of the air over Malaya, as well as the sea to the east. Their own supply lines were secure, reinforcements were pouring in, and the major land battles could begin. Their troops had been highly trained in jungle warfare, were well equipped, and many had experience of active service in China. All had a fanatical belief in their cause and considered it a privilege to die for their country. Their creed was to fight to the death and never surrender.

Admiral Sir Tom Phillips (right) with Rear-Admiral A.F.E. Palliser, his Chief of Staff. The latter remained in Singapore when 'Force Z' set off, handling intelligence and exchanging signals.

Author's collection

The Japanese troops and their air units in southern Siam consolidated their positions against weak opposition in the first few days of occupation. They also brought the war to Burma. On 9 December contingents of the 2nd Burma Frontier Force advanced into Siam from Mergui on the west coast of the Kra Isthmus, with the intention of cutting the rail line to Malaya, but were soon repulsed. On the same day Ki-27 'Kate' fighters raided the airfield at Victoria Point, the most southerly point of Burma in the Tenasserim district of the Kra Isthmus, and destroyed some light aircraft. Then troops of the 143rd Regiment of the Japanese 15th Army began advancing westwards to this airfield, but its ground personnel were evacuated by air before their arrival on 13 December. The Japanese occupation of this airfield cut the air route from Burma to Malaya, at least for short-range fighter aircraft. On 11 December Ki-27 'Kate' fighters strafed the Burmese airfield of Tavoy in the north of Kra Isthmus, and two days later fifty-one Ki-21 'Sally' heavy bombers raided Mergui airfield, between Tavoy and Victoria Point.

Despite these preliminary incursions into Burmese territory, the main objective of the Japanese for the next two months was Malaya. On 11 December two infantry regiments of the 25th Army, supported by a tank battalion and an artillery battalion, began to advance rapidly down the western road towards Jitra. A third regiment, supported by two tank companies and an artillery battery, advanced down the centre of Malaya towards Kroh.

These positions were defended by the 11th Indian Division of III Indian Corps, but without adequate weapons or preparations. Most of their anti-tank weapons were soon knocked out, while Japanese infantry infiltrated around their positions and cut off supply routes. The speed of these attacks coupled with the use of tanks overwhelmed the defenders. The depleted RAF squadrons were unable to give air support, being occupied with Japanese attacks against airfields or on standby against potential air raids on Singapore. The losses suffered by the 11th Indian Division became extremely severe, in terms of men and equipment. The demoralised and scattered survivors were forced to withdraw on 12/13 December, even though the 12th Indian Brigade was brought in to bolster defences along the Grik road on the right flank. Not all the bridges were blown during these retreats and the Japanese continued to advance.

The Japanese Army Air Force did not support ground forces in the action at Jitra but made several attacks on Georgetown on the island of Penang from 11 December onwards, resulting in considerable damage. The Buffalos of 453 (RAAF) Squadron were brought up to nearby Butterworth airfield on 13 December and succeeded in shooting down six of the attackers. But the squadron was withdrawn before Japanese troops reached Butterworth on 16 December. The troops in Penang Fortress, also part of III Indian Corps, were evacuated hurriedly by sea on the following night, leaving behind a number of coastal craft.

The battered remains of the 11th Indian Division retreated further south to Taiping on the west coast and took up new defensive positions. Consideration was given to sending one of the two brigades of the 8th Australian Division to their support, but the latter was based in Johore in the southern tip of Malaya, where it was needed to help repulse any seaborne attack on Singapore, and the proposal was rejected. However, the 12th Brigade had retreated in good order from its positions on the Grik road and was combined with the 11th Indian Division.

After these operations the whole of northern Malaya had been lost and the replacement of battle casualties was imperative. But it was estimated that two months would be required for the assembly and equipment of another army and its arrival by sea at Singapore. In the meantime it was hoped that the troops in western Malaya could somehow delay any further advance by the Japanese, perhaps on a defensive line along the Perak river to the south of their temporary positions.

On 19 December 453 (RAAF) Squadron was transferred with fifteen Buffalo fighters to Kuala Lumpur airfield in support of the defenders. The airfield came under constant air attack by the Japanese and although the Australian pilots flew courageously, their aircraft were outclassed by the A6M 'Zeros'. Only three Buffalos remained airworthy after three days of combat, and they had to be withdrawn to Singapore.

The Brewster B-339E Buffalo single-seat fighter served operationally with the RAF only in the Far East. Three RAF squadrons and one RAAF squadron were equipped with these machines when the Japanese invaded Malaya on 8 December 1941. Although the squadrons acquitted themselves well against Japanese bombers, the Buffalo was outclassed in speed and rate of climb by the Mitsubishi A6M2 'Zero'.

Author's collection

Other RAF aircraft carried out reconnaissance along the east coast to detect any movement of Japanese craft southwards. Some were spotted off Singora in Siam together with a concentration of aircraft on the nearby airfield of Sungei Patani. The latter was raided on the nights of 26 and 27 December by Blenheims of 34 Squadron with considerable success, for the loss of one Blenheim.

It was hoped that the losses suffered by the RAF and RAAF squadrons in Malaya could be made good far more quickly than those of the ground troops. The Air Ministry had already planned to provide over 150 additional aircraft, consisting of Catalinas, Blenheims and Hudsons to be flown out to Singapore, as well as Curtiss Kittyhawks and Hawker Hurricanes to be crated and dispatched by sea. The reality proved different. Three Catalinas had been flown from the Dutch East Indies on 12 December and four more arrived later from Gibraltar. Twelve Blenheims were flown from Egypt between 12 and 14 December but five were lost en route. Ten Hudsons arrived from Australia on 23 December, but of thirty-six flown from England only fifteen eventually arrived. No Kittyhawks were ever sent and fifty-one crated Hurricanes did not arrive until 13 January, too late to save the situation.

However, events in Burma seemed to offer some hope that the tide of war in the air might be turning, when the Japanese attempted to raid Rangoon in

The Mitsubishi Ki-30 light bomber, codenamed 'Ann' by the Allies, first entered service in 1938. It had a crew of two, was armed with one machine-gun firing forward and another aft, and could carry up to 882lb of bombs. Already obsolescent as an operational aircraft in December 1941, it was soon relegated to training duties but was also employed as a suicide bomber towards the end of the war.

Author's collection

The land-based Mitsubishi G4M of the Japanese Navy Air Force, codenamed 'Betty' by the Allies, was built in greater numbers than any other Japanese bomber. It normally had a crew of seven, was initially armed with five machine-guns and a 20mm cannon, carried a bomb-load of about 1,750lb, and had a range of almost 3,000 miles. However, with no protection for its fuel tanks, it was highly combustible when attacked by Allied fighters. One of the type's first exploits was a share in the sinking of *Prince of Wales* and *Repulse*, but variants served throughout the Second World War. This captured example bears USAAF markings.

Author's collection

daylight on 23 December. The total force dispatched consisted of forty-two Ki-21 'Sally' heavy bombers, twenty-seven Ki-30 'Ann' light bombers and thirty Ki-27 'Kate' single-seater fighters. They were met by fifteen Buffalos of the RAF's 67 Squadron and twelve Curtiss P-40 Tomahawks of the American Volunteer Group (AVG), which claimed thirteen bombers destroyed and seven probables, plus one fighter and one probable. Four P-40s were shot down but two pilots were saved. Despite this success in the air, the bombing caused heavy casualties among the civilian population of Rangoon.

The Japanese aircraft tried again two days later, on Christmas Day. On this occasion there were thirty-five Ki-21 'Sally' heavy bombers and twenty-seven Ki-30 'Ann' light bombers, escorted by twenty-five Ki-43 'Oscar' and thirty-two Ki-27 'Kate' fighters. Their attacks resulted in considerable damage in Rangoon and its main airfield of Mingaladon, with over 5,000 civilians killed and streams of refugees fleeing the capital. The defending P-40s and Buffalos claimed sixteen enemy bombers and twelve fighters shot down for the loss of six of their own number. These claims seem to have been exaggerated but the scale of the air raids in Burma diminished for some weeks afterwards, partly because the Japanese bombers and fighters had more urgent business in Malaya.

On 27 December Lieutenant-General Sir Henry Pownall took over as Commander-in-Chief Far East from Air Chief Marshal Sir Robert Brooke-Popham, but was faced with an impossible situation in Malaya. At this time the Japanese had resumed their push southwards. In the west they had overrun the defences along the Perak river on 26 December, partly by outflanking them with the use of seaborne landing craft. The tired and despondent troops of the 11th Indian Division were falling back to new positions around Kampar. Here, after two days of stiff fighting, the defenders were forced back yet again, to positions behind the Slim river, where they awaited a fresh onslaught.

Another threat had developed on the east coast, since two infantry regiments of the Japanese 25th Army had advanced from Kota Bharu and on 23 December reached the outskirts of Kuantan, where an important airfield was situated. This area was held by the 22nd Brigade, part of III Indian Corps' 9th Indian Division, and initial skirmishing had begun. On the night of 30/31 December the defenders demolished the airfield facilities and withdrew a few miles to the south, behind the Kuantan river running towards the coast. The Japanese attacked in force and managed to infiltrate the positions by wading across the upper reaches of the river. Some fierce fighting followed and the defenders withdrew on 2 January after losing about a third of their number.

As the distance to Singapore shortened, the Japanese resumed air attacks on the base from 30 December, mainly against the airfields and their depleted squadrons. The initial attacks took place at night but they switched to daylight bombing when it became clear that the air defences were very weak. The raiders usually went in at about 25,000 feet and within two weeks destroyed over fifty aircraft. The raids continued without respite.

On 3 January 1942 the first reinforcement convoy arrived at Singapore, bearing the 45th Indian Brigade from India. This was the first of two brigades to be sent from Bombay by General Sir Archibald Wavell, the Commander-in-Chief of India, in response to Winston Churchill's urgent request for reinforcements. The troops had been only partially trained and equipped, but the two brigades were the only forces in India readily available for Malaya. They required equipment and further training before going into action.

In the western sector the battle of the Slim river began on 5 January. Japanese tanks and infantry swept forward and crossed river bridges before these could be demolished. They soon overcame the defenders, almost wiping out some contingents. By 7 January one brigade had virtually ceased to exist and the other had been reduced to about a third of its original numbers. The survivors fell back in small units.

Japanese reinforcements arrived and their remorseless advance continued against weak opposition. Seaborne forces landed near Port Swettenham on 10 January, narrowly failing to cut off the remains of the retreating 11th Indian Division. The Japanese occupied the major town of Kuala Lumpur on the following day. The 11th Indian Division continued to withdraw and on the night of 13/14 January took up positions in the area of Kluang and Rengam. By this time the whole of central Malaya had been occupied by the enemy. The remains of the 9th and 11th Indian Divisions were presented with the task of defending the northern boundaries of Johore State and preventing the Japanese from advancing on Singapore. Together with other forces, which included battalions of the 8th Australian Division, they were dispersed across the Malayan peninsula into commands named Westforce and Eastforce.

On 13 January a second reinforcement convoy arrived at Singapore with the 53rd British Infantry Group of the 18th British Division, together with three British anti-aircraft regiments and a British anti-tank regiment. These forces had been diverted from their sea passage to the Middle East. There were also fifty-one crated Hurricanes and twenty-four pilots in the convoy. The aircraft were rapidly assembled and moved to airfields in Singapore for flight testing. It was hoped that they would establish some supremacy against Japanese fighters and also help destroy the numerous bombers that continued to raid the port and its airfields.

Meanwhile the Chiefs of Staff of the Western nations had created ABDACOM (American, British, Dutch and Australian Command) covering Malaya, Burma, the Netherlands East Indies, the Philippines and various small islands. General Wavell was given the task of commanding the new organisation and assumed his unenviable position on 15 January. It was already far too late to have any notable effect on the war against Japan and would have only a limited existence.

Even Japanese troops needed short periods of rest and there were several days of respite in Malaya while supplies and reinforcements were brought up along their extended lines in Malaya. The defenders also received another

Reinforcements of Indian troops arriving in Singapore to help resist the Japanese invasion of Malaya.

Author's collection

reinforcement on 22 January when a convoy arrived in Singapore with the 44th Indian Brigade, but unfortunately these troops proved to be no better trained than their compatriots in the 45th Indian Brigade, which had arrived on 3 January. Two days later another convoy arrived with about 1,900 Australian reinforcements, together with the 2/4th Australian Machine-Gun Battalion. The latter proved excellent but the others were simply raw recruits, many of whom had sailed within a fortnight of enlistment and had no experience of handling weapons.

Bitter fighting broke out again in the western sector when the Japanese began to advance during the night of 23/24 January, and once more the defenders were forced to withdraw. On the eastern front air reconnaissance on 26 January by two Hudsons revealed a large enemy convoy approaching Endau, about 20 miles north-east of the port. An air attack from Singapore was launched in the early afternoon by nine Hudsons and twelve Vildebeests, all carrying bombs since the sea was considered too shallow for the torpedoes normally carried by the Vildebeests. These bombers were escorted by fifteen Buffalos and eight Hurricanes. All met intense anti-aircraft fire and fighter opposition, but scored direct hits on two transports and a cruiser, while troops in barges and on the beaches were also bombed and strafed. Five Vildebeests were shot down and many of the other aircraft were damaged.

A second attack was launched in mid-afternoon by nine other Vildebeests and three Fairey Albacores of the Fleet Air Arm, escorted by twelve fighters. More hits were scored but five Vildebeests, two Albacores and one fighter were shot down. Then five Hudsons operating from Sumatra attacked the barges and troops, returning without loss. The destroyers HMS *Vampire* and HMS *Thanet* left Singapore in the late afternoon and intercepted the convoy early the following morning, engaging a Japanese cruiser and three destroyers. During the battle *Thanet* was sunk and *Vampire* was badly damaged but managed to return.

Some additional strength for the depleted fighter squadrons was achieved on 27 January when forty-eight Hurricanes were flown off the aircraft carrier HMS *Indomitable* and arrived in Singapore. These helped to replace the losses of RAF and RAAF fighters in air combat and on the ground during the numerous air raids against airfields in Singapore. However, despite its success against German fighters and bombers in the Battle of Britain, the Hurricane proved less effective in combat with the Japanese 'Zero', being slower and less manoeuvrable at heights lower than 20,000 feet. Moreover, the 'Zeros' came over in such numbers that the Hurricanes had few opportunities to tackle the Japanese bombers.

The last reinforcement convoy arrived at Singapore on 29 January, bringing the main party of the 18th British Division, consisting of its Headquarters and two Infantry Brigades. These were desperately needed but their arrival was far too late to affect the outcome of the battles on the Malayan mainland. Following their recent encounters on the ground, all the troops of Eastforce and Westforce were ordered to withdraw to Singapore. The final evacuation of Johore took

The Mitsubishi A6M single-seat fighter, codenamed 'Zero' by the Allies, first entered service with the Japanese Navy Air Force in mid-1940. Light and manoeuvrable, it outclassed Chinese aircraft and then proved superior to Allied fighters when Japan entered the Second World War. The early variant was armed with two machine-guns mounted on the upper fuselage but later variants were additionally fitted with two wing-mounted 20mm cannon. Although eventually outclassed by Allied fighters, it served throughout the war and ended as a kamikaze aircraft. It could normally carry 132lb of bombs, or 550lb on suicide missions. This captured example bears US markings.

Author's collection

place on the night of 30/31 January, although heavy losses were suffered by the defenders in their fighting retreat. The worst experience had befallen the 22nd Indian Infantry Brigade, part of the 9th Indian Division, which had been cut off in its defence of the central sector and suffered huge casualties. Without ammunition, most of the exhausted survivors had been forced to surrender and only a handful of men reached the causeway to Singapore. The remainder of the Malayan peninsula was lost in these actions and the only measure left was to defend the island of Singapore for as long as possible.

The defences of Singapore had been directed southwards towards the sea, protecting the town and its naval base. The island itself, about the size of the Isle of Wight, was bereft of defences along the beaches of the Johore Strait separating it from the mainland. The indented coastline was about 70 miles long and difficult to defend along its entire length. The garrison consisted of about 85,000 men, but many of these were normally non-combatant and thus not available for defensive operations. Of the remainder, a large number were the recently arrived recruits with little training, equipment or battle experience.

It was considered that the four airfields on the island could not be held against air and ground attack. Thus the serviceable bombers were flown across the Malacca Strait to airfields in Sumatra, from where they could still operate against the Japanese in Malaya. Only a few Hurricanes of the RAF and Fairey Swordfish of the Fleet Air Arm remained on the island, the pilots struggling against impossible odds in the continuous raids by Japanese bombers escorted by fighters. Many civilians and skilled workers were evacuated by sea to Ceylon within the first few days of January.

The Japanese forces on the mainland consisted of three divisions with supporting armour, and their General Yamashita was supplied with accurate information about the disposition of the defending units, mainly from agents on the island. The attack against Singapore began in the morning of 8 February when strong air attacks were followed by artillery bombardment and fire from machine-guns along the north-east coast. Then landing craft were seen approaching in the late evening and defensive fire was opened on them. Many troops who landed on the beaches were mown down but others managed to infiltrate round the defences and work their way inland.

The defences began to run out of ammunition and their communication lines were cut. A difficult retreat became necessary to prepared positions in the south, but fierce fighting took place for the next few days with the outcome remaining in doubt. At one time it even seemed that the Japanese troops would be defeated but fresh reinforcements were brought in from the mainland, including tanks and artillery. While these actions were taking place, the air defences of the island had been whittled down to just ten Hurricanes and four Swordfish. These flew mission after mission and accounted for several aircraft, but the Japanese strength was overwhelming.

Lieutenant-General Tomoyuki Yamashita, the commander of the Japanese 25th Army which invaded Malaya and Siam. *Author's collection*

General Wavell visited Singapore on 10 February and on his return to Java telegraphed a report to Churchill. He stated that the battle was not going well, that the Japanese were infiltrating positions, that they had command of the air, and that some of the defenders had had insufficient training and their morale was not good. A message from General Yamashita was dropped on Singapore City on 11 February calling for surrender, but no reply was given. But the defenders had been driven back to the perimeter of the city and the outcome was inevitable. The defences held for the next few days while all possible personnel were evacuated by sea. Then, at 1130 hours on 15 February, a joint deputation of military and civil leaders drove to the Japanese lines bearing a flag of truce. The Japanese demanded unconditional surrender and this took effect at 0830 hours on the following day, when the defenders laid down their arms.

The battle casualties in the Malayan campaign were listed as 38,496 British, 18,490 Australian, 67,340 Indian and 14,382 Local Volunteer Groups, giving a

Japanese air attacks on central Singapore during daylight hours on 20 and 21 January 1942 caused considerable damage. This photograph was taken in Raffles Place, the city's equivalent to London's Piccadilly Circus.

Author's collection

grand total of 138,708. Of these, over 130,000 became prisoners-of-war and then suffered barbarously cruel treatment that many did not survive. This was one of the most humiliating defeats in British history, for never before had so many of their troops surrendered on a single occasion.

A myth of Japanese invincibility was born, for Siam, Malaya and Singapore were not their only conquests since hostilities had begun. Hong Kong had fallen to them on 25 December, the Celebes on 9 February and Borneo on 10 February. Sumatra would follow on 16 February and Java on 8 March, while most of the Philippines were already under their dominion. In the cynical words of their leaders, these were to become Japan's 'Greater East Asia Co-Prosperity Sphere', but the real intention was a ruthless and cruel dictatorship. The next objective was the conquest of the whole of Burma. This would supply more oil and rice, close the American supply line to China and perhaps open the door to the Japanese occupation of India.

(*Above*) Singapore photographed shortly before the Japanese invasion. It was described as 'The key to the Indian Ocean'. (*Below*) A Chinese Military Mission, consisting of senior officers of the country's Army, Navy and Air Force, visited Malaya before the Japanese invasion. They toured the entire Malayan peninsula from the border of Siam to Singapore, inspecting the defences. In this photograph the head of the Mission, General Shang Chen, is being shown one of the latest automatic rifles.

Author's collection

(*Above*) Left to right: Air Marshal
Sir Robert Brooke-Popham
(Commander-in-Chief Far East);
General Sir Archibald Wavell;
Vice-Admiral Sir Geoffrey Layton.
Author's collection

(*Right*) Air Vice-Marshal C.M.
Pulford was appointed Air Officer
Commanding Far East on 30 April
1941. He lost his life on an
unknown date after the convoy of
small boats evacuated from
Singapore on 13 February 1942 was
attacked by Japanese warships in
the Banka Strait between Sumatra
and Java. The naval motor launch
in which he was travelling was
damaged and then beached on a
small island with almost no
sustenance.

Author's collection

(*Above*) Crews of the Royal Netherlands Indies Army's Air Division being greeted by Air Vice-Marshal Pulford on arrival with their Martin 139W bombers at Singapore on 9 December 1941.
Gerrit J. Zwanenburg, KON, MBE, collection

(*Opposite top*) A Martin 139W of the Royal Netherlands Indies Army's Air Division being bombed up in Singapore. It could carry up to 2,260lb of bombs.
Gerrit J. Zwanenburg, KON, MBE, collection

(*Opposite bottom*) Martin 139Ws of the Royal Netherlands Indies Army's Air Division in flight over Malaya, escorted by a Wirraway tactical reconnaissance aircraft on the strength of 21 (RAAF) Squadron. The Wirraway was the Australian version of the North American AT-6 trainer, known in the RAF as the Harvard. No. 31 (RAAF) Squadron was mainly equipped with Brewster Buffalo Is from August 1941 and was based at RAF Seletar in Singapore.
Gerrit J. Zwanenburg, KON, MBE, collection

The battleship HMS *Prince of Wales*, 36,700 tons displacement, leaving the Strait of Johore on 8 December 1941. She was sunk by Japanese torpedo-bombers two days later, with the loss of 327 men from her complement of 1,612.

Author's collection

The battle cruiser HMS *Repulse* leaving the Strait of Johore on 8 December 1941. She was sunk two days later by Japanese torpedo-bombers, with the loss of 612 men from her crew of 1,308.

Author's collection

Left to right: Lieutenant-General A.E.
Percival (General Officer Commanding
Malaya); Major-General H.G. Bennett
(Commander, 8th Australian Division).
Author's collection

Lieutenant-General Sir Lewis Heath
(Commander, III Indian Corps).
Author's collection

Australian troops on parade in Malaya before the Japanese invasion.

General Sir Archibald P. Wavell inspecting troops in Singapore during November 1941. He assumed Supreme Command of the Far East Forces on 15 January 1942, after the Japanese invasion of Malaya.

Author's collection

The Mitsubishi F1M floatplane, codenamed 'Pete' by the Allies, was employed by the Japanese Navy throughout the Second World War. Originally intended for short-range reconnaissance, it proved highly reliable after the prototype was modified and even saw service as a dive-bomber in amphibious operations. With a crew of two, its armament consisted of two machine-guns firing forward with another aft, and it could also carry up to 132lb of bombs.

Author's collection

The Nakajima Ki-43, named 'Peregrine Falcon' by the Japanese and 'Oscar' by the Allies, was a single-seat fighter which first entered service with the Japanese Army Air Force in 1941. Fitted with two synchronised machine-guns firing through the propeller (later replaced with two 20mm cannon), it served throughout the Second World War and Allied pilots acknowledged it as a very effective aircraft it. This example of a captured 'Oscar' carries USAAF markings.

Author's collection

The single-seat Mitsubishi A5M, codenamed 'Claude' by the Allies, was employed by the Japanese Navy as a carrier-borne fighter at the beginning of the Second World War. The early model was armed with two machine-guns but a later version was fitted with two 20mm cannon. It could also carry two 66lb bombs. Although of light construction, the machine was still capable of flying even after taking considerable punishment.

Author's collection

The three-seater Aichi E13A floatplane, known as 'Jake' to the Allies, was employed by the Japanese Navy with considerable success during the Second World War, primarily on long-range reconnaissance and escort duties. Armed with one rearward-firing machine-gun and one downward-firing 20mm cannon, it could also carry about 550lb of bombs or depth-charges. It had a range of up to 1,300 miles and could thus remain airborne for almost fifteen hours.

Author's collection

The Mitsubishi Ki-21 heavy bomber, codenamed 'Sally' by the Allies, served with the Japanese Army Air Force throughout the Second World War. It normally carried a crew of five and could be armed with up to seven machine-guns in nose, ventral and dorsal positions, with one remotely controlled in the tail. The bomb-load was 1,650lb. It was vulnerable to Allied fighters such as the Hurricane, unless escorted by fighters.

Author's collection

The first salvoes of bombs in the engagement that led to the sinking of *Prince of Wales* and *Repulse* were dropped by Mitsubishi G3Ms of the Japanese Navy Air Force's 22nd Air Flotilla based at Saigon, operating from a distance that seemed impossible to the Royal Navy. Code-named 'Nell' by the Allies, this twin-engined bomber had a range of about 2,700 miles, a crew of five, was armed with three machine-guns and carried about 1,750lb of bombs or a torpedo. However, it became obsolescent in 1943 and remaining examples were employed on reconnaissance duties or as trainers or glider-tugs.

Author's collection

Dutch, Australian and British air personnel at an airfield, giving the 'V for Victory' sign. Three squadrons of the Royal Netherlands Air Force arrived in Singapore from the Netherlands East Indies on 9 December 1941, the day after the Japanese invasion of Malaya. Their aircraft consisted of nine Brewster Buffalo fighters and twenty-two Martin 139W medium bombers. A Lockheed Hudson is in the background.

Author's collection

Lockheed Hudsons of the RAAF over Malaya in late 1941. Both 1 and 8 Squadrons of the RAAF were equipped with these aircraft as part of the country's scanty air defences.

Author's collection

Two Consolidated Catalina Is of 205 Squadron, based at Seletar in Singapore, photographed in late 1941. Three of these long-range flying boats were carrying out patrols over the southern Indian Ocean and the China Seas, hunting for the Japanese invasion fleet in the Gulf of Siam, when one of them was shot down by a Zero on 7 December 1941.

Author's collection

Men of a battalion of the Gordon Highlanders helping to construct anti-tank obstacles with tree trunks during the Japanese invasion.

Author's collection

(*Above*) Indian gunners in Malaya undergoing training with Bofors anti-aircraft guns against low-flying attacks. The vertical stakes are anti-tank devices.

Author's collection

(*Opposite top*) Infantrymen of the Argyll and Sutherland Highlanders undergoing training in Malaya to resist the Japanese invasion.

Author's collection

(*Opposite bottom*) The Mitsubishi Ki-46-III, known as 'Dinah' to the Allies, was one of the most successful army reconnaissance aircraft employed by the Japanese during the Second World War. On the Burma front it was able to fly above the ceiling of RAF fighters until the Spitfire arrived in the area. This captured aircraft was evaluated by the Allied Tactical Air Intelligence Unit of South-East Asia Command after V-J Day.

J.M. Bruce/G.S. Leslie collection

A Japanese tank knocked out by Australian forces after the invasion of Malaya on 8 December 1941. Two of the crew are lying dead in front of it.

Author's collection

CHAPTER TWO

The Attack on Burma

The Japanese had made significant gains in the Tenasserim district of southern Burma during their campaign in Malaya. Their 143rd Regiment of the 15th Army had soon occupied Victoria Point on the southern tip after attacking from southern Siam. Following an air raid, the town and airfield of Tavoy had fallen to ground attack by the 112th Regiment of the 15th Army on 19 January 1942. This had cut off the port and airfield of Mergui, and the garrison had been evacuated by sea. The garrison at Tavoy had retreated northwards to Moulmein at the mouth of the Salween river, but in turn this port and its airfield had fallen to the Japanese on 30 January. The defenders had been evacuated by sea to Rangoon, leaving the whole of Tenasserim district in the hands of the Japanese. This had not only preserved their rail link from Bangkok to Malaya but threatened another from Moulmein to Pegu, north of Rangoon, which was of strategic value in their push to conquer the whole of mainland Burma.

Meanwhile the Japanese 15th Army had been strengthened on 10 January by the arrival of its 33rd Division from China. This brought its strength up to about 35,500 battle-hardened men, together with armour and troop-carrying vehicles, commanded by the resourceful Lieutenant-General Shojiro Iida. It was supported by the 5th Air Division, commanded by Lieutenant-General H. Obata, with a total strength of over 200 aircraft. These consisted of fighters, light bombers, heavy bombers and reconnaissance aircraft. They had arrived in Siam from Formosa in early January and now concentrated on destroying the Allied air forces in Burma.

Rangoon had experienced a succession of air raids during this period and many thousands of its civilians had fled. The air defences of the country had been whittled down during these engagements. Air Vice-Marshal D.F. Stevenson, who had been appointed as Air Officer Commanding Burma at the beginning of January 1942, reported on 14 February that only thirty Allied fighters remained serviceable. These were short-range Hurricanes of the RAF, which had arrived shortly before, and P-40 Tomahawks of the American Volunteer Group. Only a single radar station was available to give advance warning of enemy aircraft heading for Rangoon. The situation with RAF bombers was equally parlous, for only six serviceable Blenheims were available at any one time, plus an Indian squadron equipped with reconnaissance Lysanders which could carry light bombs.

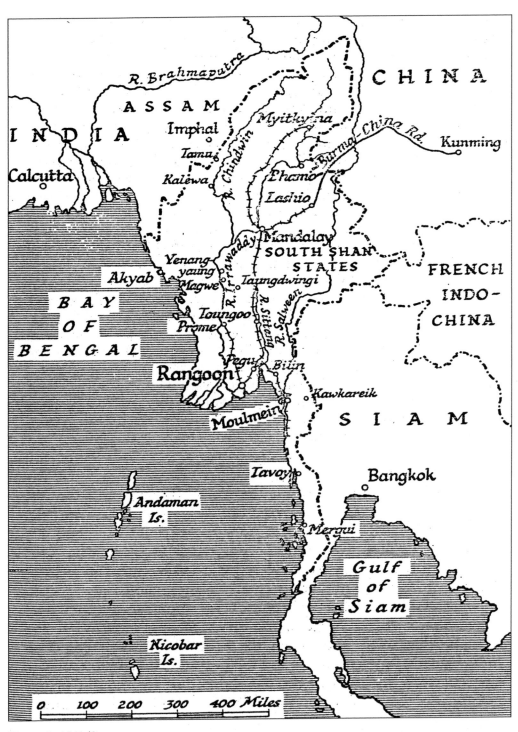

Burma in 1941/2.

The General Officer Commanding Burma was Lieutenant-General Thomas J. Hutton, who had taken over this unenviable position on 27 December 1941. There were two divisions under his command. The older was the 1st Burma Division, formed in July 1941 and commanded by Major-General J. Bruce Scott. At that time it had been believed that the most likely Japanese attack would come from the area of Chiengmai in northern Siam. Thus a regiment, three batteries and three companies were concentrated in the Southern Shan States of Burma for defensive purposes. Elsewhere there were two Burma brigades, an Indian brigade, a garrison in Rangoon and a company which had been stationed in Tenasserim before the occupation of that district by the Japanese. These scattered forces were short of artillery, engineers, signallers, medical facilities and transport units, and were a division in name only.

The other was the 17th Indian Infantry Division, which had been formed during June 1941 at Poona in the state of Bombay. Thereafter the recruits had undergone training, primarily for desert warfare in the Middle East. During the later period this division had lost many of its experienced non-commissioned officers, posted to the Middle East or to Malaya. Three of its Indian brigades from Poona had reached Burma in December 1941. But the recruits had little practical experience of handling weapons, almost no knowledge of the country or its language, and had had no jungle training. They were joined by a Burma Brigade, consisting of a mountain battery and three regiments. This division was commanded from mid-January 1942 by Major-General J.G. Smyth.

These two divisions were obviously inadequate for the task of defending Burma, a country with a population of about 17 million within roughly the same area as France combined with Belgium and the Netherlands. It was also a country of wide climatic and topographic extremes. There was a central plain, through which three major rivers flowed in a roughly north-south direction to the Gulf of Martaban. These were the Irrawaddy, with its tributary the Chindwin, the Sittang and the Salween. The country was bounded on the south-west by the Bay of Bengal, on the north-west by jungle-clad hills separating it from the Indian states of Bengal, Assam and Manipur, on the north by the Himalayas separating it from China, and on the east by hills separating it from Indo-China and Siam. The country was beset by an intense monsoon which came in from the south-west in mid-May and lasted until mid-October.

Fortunately for the defence of Burma, Generalissimo Chiang Kai-shek had offered in late November 1941 to provide support from China with his V Army commanded by Lieutenant-General Tu Yu-Ming and his VI Army commanded by Lieutenant-General Kan Li-Chu. A Chinese army was smaller than the British, being roughly equivalent to a division; similarly a Chinese division was equivalent to a brigade and a regiment to a battalion. In addition, about a third of its men were unarmed carriers. However, the Chinese troops were noted for their bravery and experience in fighting the Japanese. These two armies came under the authority of Lieutenant-General Joseph B. Stilwell, the American Chief of

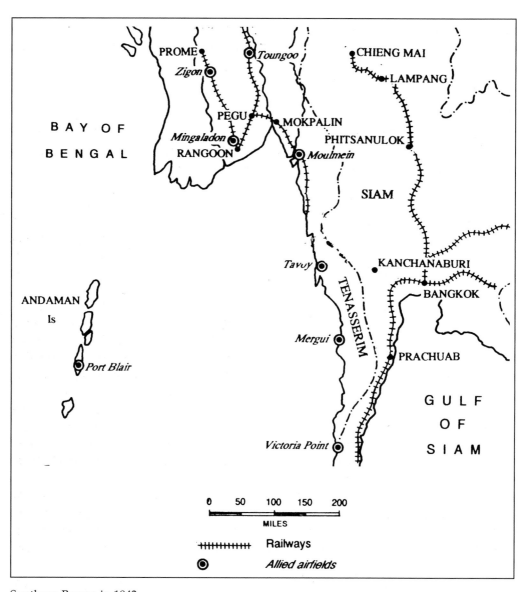

Southern Burma in 1942.

Staff to the Generalissimo. He was elderly but had the toughness of a much younger man and could speak Chinese. Nicknamed 'Vinegar Joe' for his uncompromising manner and distrust of the British, he was nevertheless a first-class leader in the field.

The Generalissimo's decision was partly motivated by the need to protect the Burma Road, which had been constructed by the Americans from Lashio in Burma across the Himalayas to Kunming in China, in order to supply military equipment. His two armies were welcome in Burma, but they were not available in their entirety for immediate dispatch. Also the route to Burma was long and tortuous, and it was difficult to carry heavy equipment. On arrival, the armies could not count on receiving further supplies from China and arrangements had to be made for their sustenance within Burma. In the event, only one division of VI Army was brought across in January 1942 and this was eventually stationed in the Shan States of Burma. During February the three divisions of V Army were still moving slowly across the mountains into Burma, hampered by lack of transport.

On 9 February the Japanese 15th Army was ordered to begin advancing as soon as possible from Moulmein to the area of Rangoon and then to prepare for a move northwards to capture the oilfields of Yenangyaung and subsequently the area of Mandalay. The 17th Indian Division held positions along the Salween river but Major-General Smyth decided that these were untenable and by 15 February withdrew his forces about 20 miles north-west to the Bilin river and set up new defences. The Japanese followed this withdrawal closely and began attacking on the following day. Very fierce fighting followed for almost four days, with attack and counter-attack, but the Japanese were far more numerous and threatened to encircle the defenders after fording the shallow river.

Another withdrawal began on the night of 19/20 February, this time towards the Sittang river. The path the troops followed with their trucks and artillery was only a rough and rutted track through the jungle. They were headed for an eleven-span bridge that had been built near Mokpalin over the broad and fast-flowing river for the railway between Moulmein and Pegu.

The Japanese employed their usual tactics of harrying retreating troops by sending a fresh party, lightly equipped and fast-moving, through the jungle on their flanks. These set up a road block between the four brigades, manned with machine-guns and mortars, and prepared to fight to the death. This road block took hours to clear, while the rear troops of the 17th Division had to turn for defence against the pursuing enemy. The men had been fighting or retreating for days, carrying their wounded and becoming so weary that they were almost asleep on their feet. They had been strafed by Japanese aircraft and once, by tragic error, by Allied aircraft. However, the leading brigades finally reached the Sittang bridge, which had been decked over to take road traffic, and on 22 February began to cross to the west bank.

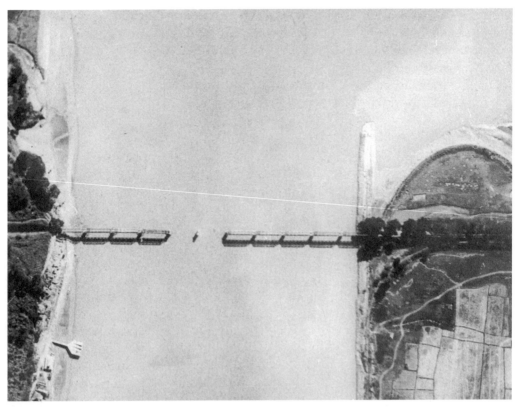

The Sittang bridge near Mokpalin, about 75 miles north-east of Rangoon, after the central spans had been blown up on 23 February 1942 on the order of the commander of the retreating 17th Indian Division. He had been informed that it was about to be seized by the Japanese, but many of his men were still trapped on the east bank.

Squadron Leader J.D. Braithwaite collection

The bridge was manned by other troops sent from Rangoon, and sappers had set demolition charges to blow it as soon as the four retreating brigades had crossed. They had also destroyed the ferries and sampans in the vicinity. In the early morning of 23 February Major-General Smyth was advised that the Japanese were pressing so hard that it was doubtful whether the bridgehead garrison on the east side of the river could hold out for more than an hour. He took the very difficult decision to blow the bridge, thus preventing it from falling into Japanese hands and providing them with a route to Rangoon. Accordingly, the bridgehead garrison withdrew to the west bank and the central spans of the bridge, each 150 feet in length, were blasted into the river.

At this there was a sudden lull in the fighting, partly because the Japanese could see that the bridge was no longer of use to them. The explosion also had an appalling effect on the troops who had not crossed. All they could do was to hold their ground for as long as possible before their ammunition ran out. Then they did their best to destroy their guns and trucks. Some men were captured by the Japanese while others tried to cross the river with the aid of logs or improvised rafts. Many tried to swim across but very few of the British and even fewer of the Indians had learnt how to swim, and the river was almost 600 yards wide. The men discarded their arms, uniforms and boots before making the attempt but many were shot or drowned in the fast current.

The outcome was catastrophic. Of approximately 8,500 men originally in the 17th Indian Division, only about 3,500 reached the west bank of the river. The majority of the other 5,000 were lost in this battle on the east bank. Moreover, only about 1,400 of the infantrymen on the west bank still carried their rifles, and there were only about 50 light machine-guns among them. The division was no longer effective as a fighting unit and withdrew about 25 miles to Pegu, where it began to re-equip and reorganise.

Despite this disaster, the destruction of the bridge resulted in a temporary halt in the Japanese advance. This was fortunate, for it enabled the deployment of the 7th Armoured Brigade under Brigadier J.H. Anstice, which had arrived in a convoy that docked at Rangoon on 21 February. About 150 Stuart and Honey tanks were brought ashore, together with carriers. Although these were only light tanks with 2-pounder guns and thin armour, their crews had had much battle experience in the Western Desert and were to prove invaluable in the next phase of the campaign in Burma. At the same time the 1st Burma Division was relieved in the Shan States by the Chinese VI Army and moved south to positions north of Pegu, while the Chinese V Army was nearing Toungoo. Nevertheless, the Japanese brought up further supplies and reinforcements, enabling their 15th Army to begin ferrying troops across the Sittang river on 2 March and then to begin advancing towards both Rangoon and Pegu, making rapid headway.

Meanwhile, heavy air raids were made against Rangoon in daylight on 25 and 26 February but the attackers suffered heavily at the hands of the RAF's Hurricanes and the Tomahawks of the AGV. About thirty-five attackers were shot down for the loss of only two defenders, but many defending aircraft were damaged and rendered unserviceable. However, it had become obvious that Rangoon could not be held against seaborne attack, for by then the Japanese Navy controlled the Bay of Bengal and the Indian Ocean. Most of the civilian population of the capital had fled or been evacuated. General the Hon. Sir Arthur Alexander arrived in the capital on 5 March to take over command from General Hutton, but General Wavell of ABDA Command had already ordered the demolition of the port area and other buildings to take place two days later. This was duly carried out and the last of the garrison set off to the north. They had to fight their way out, for the Japanese had set up a road block along their route and Alexander himself narrowly escaped capture before this was overcome.

The Japanese entered the capital at midday on 8 March, to find it deserted and burning. However, they were soon able to use the port for bringing in supplies. In contrast, the Allies were in serious difficulties. Their normal route to India had

A pilot of the American Volunteer Group (AVG) with the Chinese national emblem on his jacket, photographed during the defence of Rangoon in early 1942. The AVG had been formed in 1937 by Major C.L. Chennault, a retired officer of the US Army Air Corps, who had been an Air Adviser to the Chinese. Three squadrons were formed in China, equipped with Curtiss P-40 Tomahawks on 'lend-lease' from the USA. Generalissimo Chiang Kai-Shek agreed to the detachment of one squadron to Burma. The men were paid by the Chinese Government and received a bonus of 500 dollars for every Japanese aircraft destroyed.

Author's collection

Chinese ground staff refuelled and re-armed the Tomahawk IIAs of the American Volunteer Group (AVG). These aircraft corresponded to the Curtiss P-40B Warhawk in the US Army Air Corps, a hundred of them being diverted to the AVG in China from an order for the RAF. Powered by the Allison V-1710-33 engine giving a maximum speed of 345mph, and armed with four 0.30-inch machine-guns in the wings and two 0.50-inch machine-guns in the nose, they were a match for most Japanese aircraft. They bore the livery of shark's teeth and eyes on the engine cowlings, and the men who flew them were known as 'Flying Tigers'.

Author's collection

always been by sea, being more convenient and less expensive than building roads or railways through the jungle-clad hills which separated the two countries. Now they had no access to supplies, apart from a trickle coming in by air. Moreover, the major supply route to China via Rangoon had been cut, although the Burma Road was still open.

A reorganisation of the command structure took place on 19 March when Burma was switched from ABDACOM to come once more under General Sir Archibald Wavell, the Commander-in-Chief in India. On the same day Lieutenant-General William J. Slim arrived in Burma from Iraq to command the new 'Burcorps' under General Alexander. This consisted of its Corps Troops (including the 7th Armoured Brigade), the 1st Burma Division commanded by Major-General J. Bruce Scott, and the 17th Indian Division under Major-General D.T. Cowan (who had taken over from Major-General Smyth).

Slim was fortunate in one respect since he, Scott and Cowan were close friends who had also been comrades-in-arms. They all fought with distinction as young men in the First World War and had served together for many years in the redoubtable 6th Gurkhas. However, there was little else in their favour. Their troops had not been adequately trained for jungle warfare, the regiments were scattered and lacked equipment, and morale was poor following a succession of defeats.

Intelligence about the Japanese was almost non-existent. There was no information from Japanese prisoners and no decryption of Japanese signals giving indications of military plans. Some strategic reconnaissance of targets over Siam had been carried out by a single Blenheim converted for photographic work, but this machine had subsequently been destroyed in an air raid. On 25 January two Hurricanes modified for photo-reconnaissance work had arrived from the Middle East and these were carrying out operations over Siam, Bangkok and the airfields in the Tenasserim district. Their photographs disclosed some useful information such as numbers of enemy aircraft. Slim attempted to remedy the absence of tactical intelligence by organising mounted detachments of the Burma Military Police, but was thwarted by a shortage of ponies.

Another problem lay in the disposition of the two divisions of Burcorps, separated by about 80 miles of jungle-covered hills between the 17th Indian Division, which had retreated to defences south of Prome, and the 1st Burma Division in the Sittang valley. However, on 17 March Alexander ordered the 1st Burma Division to close the gap and it had begun moving through Toungoo, which was held by the Chinese V Army, heading for new positions about 50 miles north of Prome.

During their passage the troops had to cope with Japanese infiltrators as well as a new enemy in the form of the so-called 'Burma National Army'. This comprised young nationalists from the local population, recruited, armed, trained and controlled by the Japanese, who had assured them that the intention of the invasion was merely to hand over control once the British had been defeated. Their leader was Aung San, who had formed a group named 'The

Thirty Comrades' and was intent on forming a Burmese government. In addition to these recruits, there were bands of renegades and opportunists who preyed on small parties of troops or robbed civilians fleeing from the war zones. The division was also beginning to suffer desertions among some of its Burmese troops, who were despondent at the succession of reverses and worried about their families in areas already occupied or threatened by the Japanese.

To add to these problems, the troops of Burcorps and the Chinese armies were soon denied close support from the RAF and AVG. After the loss of Rangoon the nearest airfields from which these could operate was a small strip at Magwe, 200 miles from Rangoon, and another at Akyab, even further distant. By then, the RAF came under the command of India. Air Vice-Marshal D.F. Stevenson reported to Air Marshal Sir Richard Peirse, who had taken over as Air Officer Commander-in-Chief in India on 2 March 1942. These commanders also faced impossible odds.

The Japanese 5th Air Division had been reinforced on 18 March when aircraft from Malaya and the Netherlands East Indies flew in, bringing the total in Burma up to 420. The Allied aircraft in Burma had already been whittled down in combat and the remainder were almost obliterated within the next few days. On 21 March nine Blenheims escorted by ten Hurricanes took off from Magwe and made an effective attack on a major concentration of Japanese aircraft on Mingaladon airfield near Rangoon. This action stirred up a hornets' nest, for there was an immediate retaliation by Japanese bombers and fighters on the same day and the next. There were no dispersal facilities at Magwe airstrip and many Tomahawks, Hurricanes and Blenheims were destroyed on the ground. The few remaining RAF aircraft were withdrawn to Akyab while the AVG Tomahawks flew to Lashio and thence to China.

Then it was the turn of Akyab airfield, which received heavy air attacks on 23, 24 and 27 March, destroying more machines on the ground. The handful of RAF aircraft left were withdrawn further to Chittagong in India, thereafter using Akyab only as a forward landing ground. This left the troops in Burma almost bereft of air cover, causing considerable resentment among the men of Burcorps in the next few months. They were not aware that the depleted RAF squadrons were unable to fulfil this function from so great a distance.

At the same time a ferocious battle was taking place on the approaches to Toungoo, which was held tenaciously by the 200th Division of the Chinese V Army. The result hung in the balance for several days until the Japanese were able to bring up reinforcements. This happened soon after they consolidated their control of the Bay of Bengal, partly by occupying the Andaman Islands on 23 March and using the airfield at Port Blair. The sea passage was far more effective than the difficult land route from Siam to Burma. A major Japanese convoy, bringing in the 56th Division, arrived at Rangoon on 25 March. The division was rushed to the Toungoo area and the assault intensified, coupled with attacks from the air.

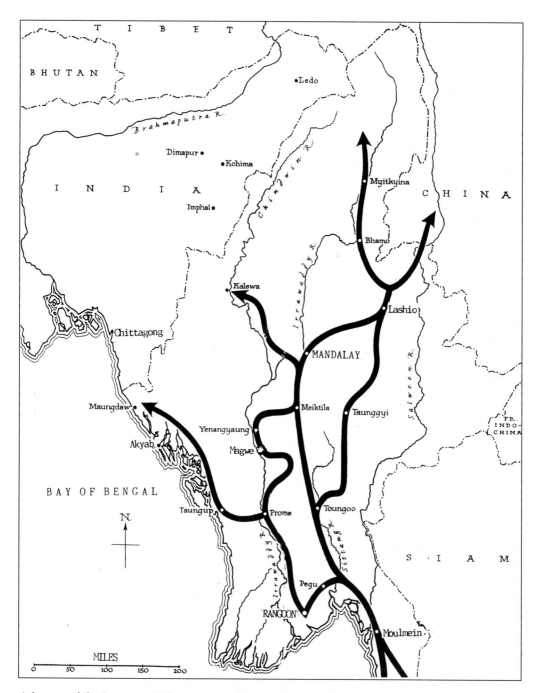

Advance of the Japanese 15th Army into Burma, January–May 1942.

Lieutenant-General Stilwell attempted to draw in reinforcements from the north but the Chinese commanders would not comply with his orders without confirmation from the Generalissimo. Stilwell appealed for diversionary attacks from Burcorps, which by this time was wholly based in the Prome area. This ancient city, with a history that dated back to the fifth century, was being bombed almost daily. The Japanese bombers came over unopposed and in perfect formation during early mornings, pattern-bombing by dropping their loads simultaneously and destroying swathes of buildings. Nevertheless, Slim did his best to comply with Stilwell's request by attacking southwards, achieving some success against the odds but suffering casualties and loss of equipment in counter-attacks.

Despite these efforts, the Chinese 200th Division in Toungoo lost about 3,000 men in the conflict. The remainder became surrounded and on 30 March the survivors were forced to split up into small parties and break out to the north, leaving most of their guns, trucks and equipment behind. They were unable to destroy the bridge over the Sittang river at Toungoo, leaving the Japanese with access to the Kachin Hills and the Shan States to the north-east. Lieutenant-General Slim later wrote, 'The loss of Toungoo was in fact a major disaster.'

Lieutenant-General Iida saw his opportunity and acted immediately. His troops and their armour swarmed across the bridge and headed towards Lashio, intent on cutting the Burma Road to China and at the same time turning the left flank of the Allied defences. It seemed that Mandalay and the whole of northern Burma might be within their reach. On 3 April Mandalay suffered a very heavy air raid. About three-fifths of the beautiful wooden houses of this city, the former home of Burmese kings, were smashed and burnt, while casualties among civilians were estimated at about 2,000 killed.

Burma was also affected in this period by other disasters, this time at sea. On 1 April a Japanese fleet named the Malaya Force left the captured port of Mergui in the Kra Isthmus in order to attack shipping off the eastern coast of India. This fleet consisted of six cruisers, eleven destroyers and a light fleet carrier, under the command of Admiral Osawa. Allied merchant ships were sailing off this coast in unescorted convoys and became easy prey for the warships, which sank nineteen vessels in a few hours on 6 April. The Japanese fleet then withdrew to Singapore.

This action was combined with a much larger foray by the Japanese Navy. It was carried out by the First Air Fleet commanded by Vice-Admiral C. Nagumo, who had been responsible for the devastating attack on the US Navy Fleet Base at Pearl Harbor in the Hawaiian Islands on 7 December 1941. The fleet left the Celebes on 28 March and headed for Ceylon. It consisted of five fleet carriers, four battleships, three cruisers, eleven destroyers and various supply ships.

Ceylon was where the newly formed Eastern Fleet of the Royal Navy was based under the command of Admiral Sir James Somerville, who had arrived in Colombo on 28 March. This was not a satisfactory fleet, having been cobbled together to meet an emergency, partly with five ancient battleships left over from

Admiral Sir James
Somerville, who assumed
command of the newly
formed Eastern Fleet based
in Ceylon on 28 March 1942.
Author's collection

the First World War. There were also seven cruisers, four of which were very old, and sixteen destroyers, mostly in need of refits. Three fleet carriers were provided, but their aircraft were inferior in performance to the Japanese. These warships had never operated together as a fleet and at the time of the emergency were scattered around the Indian Ocean.

Somerville had been warned of the approach of the Japanese fleet and this was confirmed on 4 April by a sighting from a Catalina flying boat. He prudently kept his vulnerable battleships out of the area but attempted to manoeuvre his fleet carriers to carry out a night strike. Colombo received a heavy air raid from carrier-borne Japanese aircraft in the early morning of 5 April. These made low-level and diving attacks on the port and airfield, followed by high-level attacks. The destroyer HMS *Tenedos* and the armed merchant cruiser HMS *Hector* were both hit and sank in port. Hurricanes and Fairey Fulmars engaged the attackers and claimed nineteen shot down but lost nineteen of their own number, as well as six Fairey Swordfish that happened to run into enemy fighters.

Later the same day Japanese dive-bombers succeeded in sinking the cruisers HMS *Cornwall* and HMS *Dorsetshire* south of Ceylon, with the loss of 424 men, although 1,122 survivors were picked up. Four days later the old carrier HMS

The light aircraft carrier HMS *Hermes*, 10,950 tons displacement, was completed in 1923. She had a complement of about 700 men and carried twelve aircraft. She was sunk on 9 April 1942 off Ceylon by bombers from four Japanese aircraft carriers.

Author's collection

Hermes and the destroyer RAN *Vampire* were also sunk by dive-bombers, with the loss of 315 men but with over 600 survivors picked up. Admiral Nagumo was satisfied with these results and turned his fleet back to the Malacca Strait.

These naval operations created alarm among the Allies, with the prospect of the invasion of Ceylon and the Indian sub-continent, and caused them to divert ground and air forces to their defence. They had also acted as a cover for another convoy of about forty ships which arrived at Rangoon on 7 April, bringing the 18th Division plus further supplies for the Japanese 15th Army. The Japanese division headed for the Prome area in order to increase pressure on Burcorps, already fighting against huge odds.

Although the two divisions of Burcorps at Prome were at last unified, there were serious shortages of equipment among the infantry. Their positions could no longer be held and Alexander had already decided that the only course of action for Burcorps was a retreat northwards along the Irrawaddy river, partly by using river transport. The next major defence line would be south of the oilfields of Yenangyaung, the great prize that the Japanese wanted to capture.

In the meantime the Japanese had begun launching attacks on the 17th Indian Division at Prome and, after confused fighting, had managed on 2 April to bypass some of the defences. This fighting took place in the 'Dry Belt', a dusty area of intense heat and dry watercourses. The Allied troops were exhausted after this fighting but managed to begin retreating northwards in good order. Fortunately the Japanese were also exhausted and for once did not follow up closely, although there were frequent attacks from the air. By 8 April Burcorps had reached the area south of Yenangyaung, setting up headquarters at Magwe, and Slim turned his force to face the enemy once more. It was expected that the Chinese V Army would send a regiment to take over the east end of their line but what eventually appeared was no more than a small and ill-equipped battalion.

The Japanese brought up four regiments for their assault on Yenangyaung and their patrols first made contact with Burcorps on 10 April. The battle which followed was one of the fiercest in the campaign. The first major assault took place on the night of 11/12 April, the enemy coming forward fanatically and in strength, but it was repulsed with heavy losses by infantry supported by tanks of the 7th Armoured Brigade. This attack was repeated on the following night, with the same result. However, reinforcements for the Japanese streamed up from Rangoon, while Burcorps could not make good its losses. The 1st Burma Division on the east flank was driven back on 15 April and the Chinese on the

Oil wells around a pagoda in Yenangyaung, photographed before the Japanese invasion. These oil wells made a huge contribution to the Burmese economy. They were blown up by the retreating British but eventually the Japanese were able to get the rigs back into production.

Jane Kirk collection

west flank also fell back. The oilfields were threatened and Slim visited Yenangyaung on the same day. Demolition charges had been accurately set under the supervision of an official of the oil company, W.L. Forster, and Slim now ordered them to be blown. Millions of gallons of crude oil went up, with flames rising to over 500 feet, and the installations were destroyed. A great pall of black smoke hung over Yenangyaung as a backdrop to the desperate fighting, much of it hand-to-hand.

The 17th Indian Division and the 7th Armoured Brigade stood firm but the 1st Burma Division was forced back and surrounded. Fortunately help arrived in the form of the 113th Regiment of the Chinese LXVI Army, which had begun to enter Burma on orders from Chiang Kai-shek. This regiment was part of the 38th Division commanded by Lieutenant-General Sun Li-jen, which had reached Mandalay and had been ordered to come under the command of Burcorps.

Slim planned to attack the Japanese positions from the east, with the support of tanks and artillery from the 7th Armoured Brigade, while the 1st Burma Division attacked from the south. Meanwhile, Major-General Bruce Scott managed to find a gap in the Japanese positions. His men of the 1st Burma Division were depleted in number, exhausted and almost out of ammunition, but Scott led them through the gap. They had to abandon most of their transport but passed through Yenangyaung, still in flames, and then moved northwards.

The Chinese went into their first main attack on 19 April, with the support of tanks and artillery. They made some progress and attacked again on the following day, dislodging the Japanese from some of their positions. During the night it was discovered that ambulances carrying wounded from the 1st Burma Division had not been able to join their comrades. All the wounded within them had been killed by the Japanese, bayoneted to death or their throats cut.

Slim hoped to resume attacking but more bad news from the east caused several changes of plan. Following their success at Toungoo, the Japanese had routed the Chinese VI Army in the Shan States, causing it to disintegrate. Chinese armies consisted primarily of infantry, without the support of tanks and heavy artillery such as those employed by the Japanese. By 21 April the surviving remnants were making their way back to China in small parties. The Japanese were exploiting their advantage by making with all speed for Lashio, from where the Burma Road had been constructed over the mountains to Kunming. Moreover, the Chinese V Army had suffered severe losses south of Mandalay and all communication from it had ceased. It was later learnt that its depleted divisions were making for this city, where a division of the Chinese LXVI Army was already based.

General Alexander ordered Burcorps to retreat to Mandalay and take up positions on the north side of the Irrawaddy, with the Chinese 38th Division and the 7th Armoured Brigade covering its right flank in the area of Meiktila. It was recognised that the campaign in Burma was lost and that a fighting retreat to

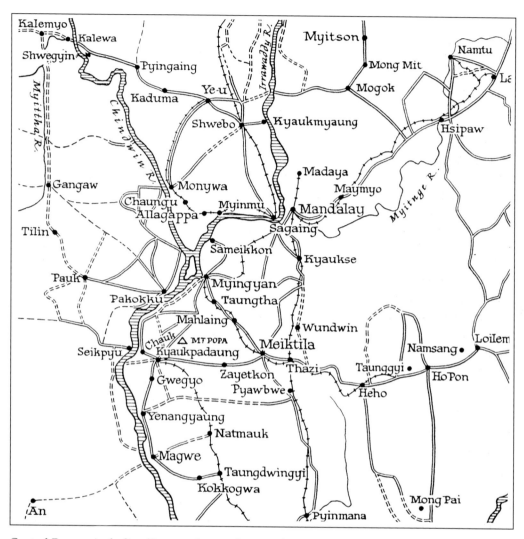

Central Burma, including Burcorps' area of retreat from Mandalay to Kalewa in May 1942.

The bridge over the Irrawaddy at Ava, about 10 miles south-west of Mandalay, was blown by the retreating British Army on 30 April 1942 to impede the advancing Japanese. Two spans fell into the river and created a sandbank.

Squadron Leader J.D. Braithwaite collection

India and China had become inevitable. The retreat to Mandalay began on 25 April and the men fought their way to the city, repulsing several attacks from the Japanese. The formations began crossing over the huge Ava bridge, close to Mandalay, while one brigade formed a rearguard on the south side. This rearguard finally crossed in darkness on 30 April and the central spans of the bridge were blown a minute before midnight, leaving the Japanese in frustration on the south side.

Lashio had been occupied by the Japanese on 29 April and the final retreat from Burma had become urgent. The spirits of the retreating troops rose, for they believed that salvation awaited them in India or China. Yet there were long and exhausting treks ahead. It was essential not only that they should keep ahead of the Japanese forces trying to overtake them but also that they should be clear of the country before the monsoon broke in mid-May. This would flood rivers and streams and make jungle tracks almost impassable.

It was originally planned that Burcorps, together with the Chinese 38th

Division from the LXVI Army and the remnants of the Chinese 22nd Division from the V Army, should make for Assam in India. However, Stilwell insisted that the two Chinese divisions should act as rearguard for the remnants of other Chinese forces still straggling northwards. Thus Slim made plans solely for Burcorps. The main route took the 17th Indian Division and most of the 7th Armoured Brigade north-west from Mandalay along a rough cart track through Ye-u and Kaduma. From there they would enter a malarial jungle and pass through Pyingaing (known as 'Pink Gin') in order to reach the Chindwin river at Shwegyin. This route included narrow bends, steep gradients and difficult streams. Slim ordered an advance party of vehicles and Royal Engineers to make the journey, doing what they could to improve the track and stock it with supplies of water for the main party.

The 1st Burma Division and a regiment of tanks had already been ordered to head west to the Chindwin at Monywa, which was held by only a small garrison of its troops. Once there they should resist any attempt by the Japanese to move northwards up the Chindwin to block the crossing at Shwegyin. They would then move north and join their comrades to be ferried by steamers across the river. From Kalewa there would be another long trek through the malarial jungle of the Kabaw Valley to the border with India and finally to Imphal.

However, the Japanese managed to move up the Chindwin in naval launches and overwhelmed the garrison at Monywa shortly before the arrival of the main division. A bitter fight followed on 2 May, in which the 1st Burma Division inflicted severe casualties on the Japanese and also destroyed many launches by mortar fire. It then began a gradual retreat northwards. At the urgent request of Alexander, the RAF provided some welcome help, since this area was within the range of their small force of medium bombers in India. The Blenheims of 113 Squadron had been detached to airfields in Assam from their base at Asansol in Bengal. Between 3 and 5 May these aircraft made a series of very effective strikes against the Japanese naval craft moving up the Irrawaddy and Chindwin.

By 8 May most of Burcorps had gathered at Shwegyin and the crossing began. However, there was enormous congestion, not only of troops with their lorries and armament but also of fleeing civilians and an accumulation of their discarded vehicles. Only six steamers were available as ferries, and embarkation and disembarkation took much time. Slim ordered one of the Burma brigades to move to the north and make a separate crossing, which it did successfully. Other troops formed defensive positions about 2 miles to the south and also threw a floating boom across the river. Japanese soldiers were appearing on both banks, having arrived by route march or been brought up by launches, and were making attacks. Their aircraft were also making occasional raids on Shwegyin.

It became apparent that the tanks and most of the heavy artillery of the 7th Armoured Brigade could never be transported. There was only one course of action. On the evening of 10 May they opened an enormous bombardment on the Japanese positions, expending all their ammunition before burning the tanks and destroying the other weapons. The troops then crossed on the steamers, which were destroyed on the other side of the river.

While these events were taking place, Lieutenant-General Sun Li-jen decided to head westwards with his 38th Division of the Chinese LXVI Army. This fought an engagement with the Japanese but two of its regiments managed to cross the upper Chindwin and reach Imphal on 24 May. The other fought a rearguard action and the survivors did not arrive until the end of the month. Meanwhile the remnants of the 22nd and 96th Divisions of the Chinese V Army withdrew to the north. The 96th managed to avoid the Japanese and reach China but the 22nd was cut off and turned north-west through the very difficult Hukawng Valley. It eventually reached Ledo in India at the end of July.

Stilwell was on his way to Myitkyina when he learnt that the Japanese had cut off the access to China. He abandoned his transport and, together with his small party, made his way on foot westwards to India. On one occasion they travelled by raft down a river and eventually reached the Chindwin. They reached Assam on 15 May and he made a characteristic comment: 'I claim we took a hell of a beating.'

It was not only troops who were seeking shelter in India and China. There were streams of civilian refugees, mainly Indians and Burmese but some British, who were fleeing from the menace of Japanese occupation and clogging the roads and tracks. The number was estimated at 400,000, of whom 10,000 did not survive. For some of them there was the godsend of unexpected and remarkable aircraft. These were Douglas DC-2 and DC-3 transports, as well as their more modern variants known as DC-47 Skytrains by the USAAF and Dakota IIIs by the RAF. They equipped the RAF's 31 Squadron and the USAAF's 2nd Troop Carrier Squadron, operating from Dinjan in northern Assam. The crews had already flown supplies to airfields in central Burma, returning with some refugees and wounded servicemen, but now they turned their attention to those streaming northwards. They flew on numerous missions to Myitkyina and took on board as many passengers as possible, not only troops with their sick and wounded but civilian men, women and children.

The efforts of these two overworked squadrons were magnificent. By the time the Japanese occupied Myitkyina on 8 May, the total number of passengers flown out was counted as 8,616. In the same period and afterwards they also dropped numerous supplies to the columns, often rice contained in three sacks one within another to prevent bursting. Other sacks contained tins of corned beef, condensed milk and fruit.

After leaving Kalewa, the men of Burcorps set off on a 90-mile march through the Kabaw Valley, known as 'Death Valley' for the virulent malaria carried by its mosquitoes. Their next objective was Tamu, an Indian town on the border of Burma south-east of Imphal. The monsoon came slightly early that year, on 12 May, bringing torrential rain from the south-east and turning the track into squelching mud. This added to their exhaustion but had one advantage, for it brought the pursuing Japanese troops to a halt and grounded their tactical aircraft on most days.

Some of these men had fought and retreated for almost a thousand miles, the longest distance in British history. Most of the units were reduced to fractions of their original numbers. The men wore ragged uniforms and many had grown beards after losing their razors. Most had lost stones in weight while some of the Indians had discarded their worn-out boots and trudged along on their bare feet. Nevertheless Slim watched the rearguard arrive on 19 May and was proud to see that they still kept their ranks and carried their arms. He later wrote, 'They might look like scarecrows but they looked like soldiers too.'

Lieutenant-General Shojiro Iida, the commander of the Japanese 15th Army which invaded Burma.

Author's collection

(*Above*) Lieutenant-General Thomas J. Hutton, the General Officer Commanding Burma from 27 December 1941 to 5 March 1942.

Author's collection

(*Opposite top*) This Indian Mountain Battery in a frontier region of Burma was photographed after the Japanese occupation of French Indo-China in mid-1940 and the invasion of Siam and Malaya on 8 December 1941. It seemed that Burma could be the next objective. Mechanised transport in the rugged and jungle-covered terrain was considered impossible, and the guns were carried on mules imported from Texas.

Author's collection

(*Opposite bottom*) In 1942 the main railway line from Rangoon ran north to Mandalay and then on to Myitkyina. A branch line ran from Mandalay north-west to Lashio. The Burma Road had been cut from Lashio through the mountains to Kunming, enabling American supplies to be carried to the Chinese forces fighting the Japanese invaders of their country. Efforts were being made to supplement the Burma Road with a railway. This photograph shows Chinese workers cutting a shelf alongside the river Nat-ting for the railway extensions.

Author's collection

(*Above*) The RAF's Photographic Section in retreat over the Irrawaddy north of Rangoon in early April 1942. The oilfields at Yenangyaung, in the background, were destroyed by the British shortly before they were occupied by elements of the Japanese 33rd Army.

Alan Fox collection

(*Opposite top*) Chinese troops entering a village in northern Burma, photographed in 1942.

Author's collection

(*Opposite bottom*) A Chinese infantryman with fixed bayonet, partly camouflaged with foliage in his webbing, advancing along a Burmese roadside.

Author's collection

(*Above*) Air Marshal Sir Richard Peirse, who took over as Air Officer Commander-in-Chief India and Ceylon on 2 March 1942.

Author's collection

(*Opposite*) An emergency dressing station was set up in April 1942 at Pyinmana, near the Salween river, about halfway between Rangoon and Mandalay, where the Chinese V Army was retreating from the advancing Japanese. Dr Gordon Seagrave, an American serving with this Chinese Army, was photographed while doing his utmost to cope with an impossible situation.

Author's collection

General Joseph Stilwell, the American commander of the Chinese V Army, armed only with a stick, leading his headquarters team out of Burma to escape the Japanese. They left Wuntho in the far north on 1 May 1942 and moved westwards for 140 miles through tortuous jungle before arriving in Assam fourteen days later. Stilwell was over 60 years of age at the time.

Author's collection

Chapter Three

Gathering Strength

During five and a half months of fighting and retreat, the Allied forces in Burma suffered casualties recorded as totalling 13,463, of which 4,033 were killed or wounded and the remainder missing. Of course, many of the 'missing' were probably prisoners, while others may have been deserters who vanished of their own accord. The Japanese casualties were recorded as 4,597 killed or wounded, and this appears to have been accurate. Losses of aircraft were almost equal at 116 Allied and 117 Japanese, either shot down in flight or destroyed on the ground.

About 10,000 troops from Burcorps eventually reached Imphal, bringing with them only 28 guns from the 150 they originally possessed, plus 50 lorries and 3 jeeps. Only about 2,000 of these men were fit for further duty. The others were suffering from illnesses contracted primarily from the jungles through which they had to pass, mainly malaria and dysentery.

Unfortunately facilities for these new arrivals were almost completely absent. Imphal was a frontier town on the end of a rickety transport system about 1,000 miles distant from Calcutta, and it had already been swamped with streams of civilian refugees from Burma. There were very few medical resources and no accommodation was immediately available. Those men from Burcorps who remained fit were told to bivouac in nearby hills but were not given tentage, ground-sheets or even blankets. They had to make shift for themselves in the streaming rain until accommodation became available, while the sick were transported elsewhere. Eventually billets for them were found in houses and other buildings which had been vacated by terrified civilians after Imphal had been bombed by the Japanese on 10 and 16 May.

On 20 May 1942 all the units from Burma were officially incorporated within IV Indian Corps of India's Eastern Command, while General Alexander relinquished his command and departed for other duties. The IV Indian Corps consisted of the 70th British Division and the 23rd Indian Division, and was under the command of Lieutenant-General N.S.M. Irwin. General Sir Archibald Wavell had reformed his Indian Command on 21 April 1942 into three separate armies. These were the Northwestern, with its headquarters at Rawalpindi, the Southern, with its headquarters at Bangalore, and the Eastern, with its headquarters at Ranchi in the state of Bihar.

As the most likely to be attacked by the Japanese, the Eastern Command under Lieutenant-General Sir Charles Broad was responsible for the defence of the states of Assam, Bengal, Orissa and Bihar. Lieutenant-General Slim was given command of its XV Indian Corps, consisting of the 14th Indian Division and the 26th Indian Division. He was joined by some of his old troops from the 1st Burma Division, for Lieutenant-General Irwin decided not to retain Burmese within his IV Indian Corps. In fact, there were very few of these Burmese troops left, for in the final stages of the retreat each man had been offered three months' pay, as well as a rifle with 50 rounds, with the suggestion that he should go back to his village and await the return of the Allies. Most had accepted and eventually became members of the resistance movement which began to harry the Japanese occupiers of their country.

Although they had impressive titles, the ground forces available for the defence of India were still weak, consisting partly of raw troops who had received little training, while modern equipment and armament was sparse. Very little support was available from the RAF, commanded by Air Vice-Marshal D.F. Stevenson, which was still woefully short of aircraft and squadrons, particularly in the Bengal region, which had 221 Group for bombers and 224 Group for fighters. In June 1942 there was not a single heavy bomber squadron in that state. There was one medium bomber squadron with Hawker Hurricanes and one with Curtiss Mohawks, which were outclassed by the Japanese 'Zeros'. There was one transport squadron, equipped with Douglas DC-2s and DC-3s. For reconnaissance there were two squadrons of Lockheed Hudsons. Moreover, there were few all-weather airfields in forward locations, although a very large programme of building had been authorised and was under way with all possible speed.

The problem of supply of material and reinforcement of personnel from the UK was exacerbated by the advance of the Afrika Korps in the Western Desert. This had become so ominous that it appeared possible that the whole of the Middle East might fall into the hands of the Axis powers. For the time being the Far East was denied major reinforcements of warships, troops and aircraft while this battle was being fought.

Wavell had already attempted to conceal all the defects within India from the Japanese by means of a deception plan. He had asked for the assistance of Major R.P. Fleming (known after the war as the journalist, explorer and author Peter Fleming), who had carried out successful deception measures during the British withdrawal from Norway in 1940. Fleming arrived in India during March 1942 and devised Operation 'Error'. Papers containing false information about formidable military defences built up in India had been planted in a staff car on the north side of the Ava bridge shortly before this was blown on 30 April, together with some of General Alexander's personal effects.

It was not known by the Allies if these documents were discovered by the Japanese and caused them to defer any advance on Assam, or whether it was solely the monsoon that stopped them. It seems more probable that it was neither. The India–Burma frontier had been designated before the war by the Japanese as the north-western limit of their so-called Greater East Asia Co-Prosperity Sphere. Their 15th Army was ordered to consolidate its conquest in Burma and to take up a defensive position. In the event, the Allies in India were given time to reorganise and build up forces for both defence and attack. Fleming remained in India and worked in its Military Intelligence Directorate, creating an inter-Service section entitled GSI (d) and having direct access to the Commander-in-Chief.

Despite all the adverse circumstances, the Allied commanders had some reasons to hope that they could eventually gain the upper hand in Burma. These included developments in intelligence. On the ground there was the new 'V' Force, formed by General Wavell in April 1941 from the hill people who lived along the border of Assam with Burma. About 2,000 tribesmen were recruited, together with about 200 British officers. The original intention was to engage in guerrilla operations in the event of a Japanese invasion of India, but since this did not materialise the main function of 'V' Force became the provision of intelligence relating to Japanese troop movements.

Of more immediate value was the RAF. During March 1942 a new Photographic Intelligence Unit had been set up in India, consisting of a Photographic Library, a Central Interpretation Section and a School of Photographic Interpretation. This was being developed when the RAF's Photographic Section escaped from Burma. On 10 April 1942 all the sections were formed into No. 5 Photographic Reconnaissance Unit at RAF Pandeveswar in Bengal. This acquired five North American B-25C Mitchells on 13 May, originally intended to be flown to the Netherlands East Indies but converted in Karachi by installing cameras and extra fuel tanks. A highly experienced officer, Wing Commander S.G. 'Bill' Wise, arrived three days later to command the unit. It moved to RAF Dum-Dum, near Calcutta, and then Hurricane IIIs began to arrive, fitted with extra fuel tanks and cameras for medium-range photography. The unit was renumbered 3 PRU and began to carry out invaluable work over Burma and beyond.

The USAAF also began to achieve a remarkable success. In April 1942 Lieutenant-Colonel William D. Old had experimented by flying a Douglas transport aircraft over the Himalayas from India to China, a route which hitherto had been considered impracticable owing to the altitude, the extreme turbulence caused by cumulo-nimbus clouds and the absence of any facilities for forced landings below. During the summer of 1942 the US Ferry Command flew 13,000 Chinese troops over this air bridge from China to train with Stilwell's force in India, throughout the monsoon period. In addition, it carried precious supplies to the Chinese armies in their own country. The route became known to the aircrews as the 'Hump Run' and RAF Dakota squadrons eventually joined in this dangerous service.

At the same time Chinese troops in Yunnan also continued training, although they did not come under Stilwell's direct command. They were known as

Group Captain S.G. 'Bill' Wise CBE, DFC*, who arrived in India as a Wing Commander to command the RAF's No. 3 Photographic Reconnaissance Unit from 16 May 1942. He had previously flown with 1 PRU in the UK and also commanded 248 Squadron, a Coastal Command strike squadron equipped with Beaufighters. He commanded the Photographic Reconnaissance Force of Air Command, South-East Asia, when it was formed on 1 February 1944. His term of command continued until 9 June 1945.

The late Group Captain S.G. Wise

Flying Officer F.D. Proctor standing in front of a Spitfire PR IV at RAF Dum-Dum, near Calcutta. This was one of the first two Spitfires to arrive at 3 PRU, ferried from the Middle East in October 1942. The unit became 681 Squadron on 25 January 1943, and Proctor commanded the squadron from December 1943 to April 1945.

The late Wing Commander F.D. Proctor

Hurricane PR IIC serial BN125, which arrived in October 1942 from the Middle East to join 3 PRU at RAF Dum-Dum in Bengal. The cameras were housed in the fairing below the fuselage. The aircraft was painted in royal blue, with wing and tail markings outlined in yellow, but the fuselage roundels were painted over.

The late Wing Commander F.D. Proctor

Ground crews of the RAF's 3 PRU at Pandeveswar in India, photographed in May 1942 in front of one of the North American B-25C Mitchells acquired from the Military Aviation Arm of the Royal Netherlands Indies Army.

Alan Fox collection

'Force X', while those in India were 'Force Y'. It was intended that both would join in the reconquest of Burma. Stilwell had said, 'We got run out of Burma and it is humiliating as hell. I think we ought to find out what went wrong, go back and take it.' He intended to be one of the leaders in this achievement.

Slim occupied part of his time with the intensive training of the men in his new command, particularly the inexperienced men of the 26th Indian Division commanded by Major-General T.G.G. Heywood, as well as those in his head-quarters staff. He concentrated on mobility and marksmanship. Every man had to learn how to limit his kit to the minimum and move rapidly through terrain at short notice. The Japanese had often employed the tactic of infiltrating around troops on the march and setting a road block ahead of them. One way to defeat this would be for specially trained troops to hook round the road block and take it from the rear. But the British and Indian troops had yet to learn how to move through the jungle.

On the other hand Slim's 14th Indian Division, commanded by Major-General W.L. Lloyd, was already responsible for the defence of the southern part of Assam and Bengal against any Japanese invasion from Burma. This area included the northern border of Burma's Arakan district and also the Sunderbans of India. The latter was the delta region where the waters of the Ganges, Brahmaputra and Hoogly rivers entered the Bay of Bengal.

It seemed possible that a seaborne incursion would be made up the Hoogly river in order to capture the major town of Calcutta. Slim attempted to obtain craft and marines from the Navy, without success, and decided to improvise. He managed to acquire about a hundred vessels. These included fast motor boats, small steamers in which 2-pounder and anti-tank guns were installed, and larger steamers for transport. They were crewed by enthusiastic volunteers from the Inland Water Transport Service. Although most of the vessels were old and the flotilla was only makeshift, there was no doubt about the fighting spirit of these men.

Perhaps the most important requirement for the Allies at this time was an improvement in morale. This was given a boost after the Battle of Midway in the central Pacific, which took place between American and Japanese aircraft carriers. On 4 June 1942 four major Japanese carriers were sunk by American naval bombers, for the loss of one American carrier which was badly damaged and sank very slowly but with little loss of life. This victory proved a shattering blow to the Japanese Navy and its Naval Air Force. Their leaders began to realise that they had awoken a sleeping giant by their attack on Pearl Harbor. The immense industrial strength and technical expertise of the USA was marshalled to the war effort, while millions of her population joined the armed services. The Japanese were to prove unable to match this tremendous effort.

The naval victory at Midway also had its effect on the defence of India, for it became apparent that a Japanese invasion of Ceylon was now less likely. Thus it became far less important for Wavell to build up his Southern Army and he was able to concentrate on the probable theatre of war, the border of Assam with Burma. However, the defeat of the Japanese at sea did not convince the Allied troops on the ground that they could beat them in the jungle. In the mind of the average British soldier, the Japanese enemy had been transformed from a sort of comic character into a superman who could move with ease through impossible terrain, live for days on a handful of rice, and always fight with intense dedication and ferocity. One man who had arrived in India shortly after the fall of Rangoon, on the recommendation of the War Office, was determined to destroy this myth. This was Lieutenant-Colonel Orde C. Wingate.

Lieutenant-General Slim described Wingate as 'A strange, excitable, moody creature, but he had fire in him. He could ignite other men.' He certainly had a proven record of success in guerrilla operations against the Arabs in Palestine before the war and then in Abyssinia against the Italians. After studying the situation in Burma, he made an unorthodox military proposal to Wavell. This was the creation of a Long Range Penetration Group (LRPG) which would operate deep behind Japanese lines and disrupt communications, blow up bridges and supply dumps, and gather intelligence. Such a plan was not novel, for cavalry regiments had been employed in this way in the past, but Wingate's method of

Brigadier Orde Charles Wingate, who commanded the special force known as the Long Range Penetration Group (or Chindits) which first set out in several columns on 7 February 1943 from Imphal in Manipur to operate 170 miles behind Japanese lines in northern Burma. Born in 1903, he died on 24 March 1944 after his second expedition, when the aircraft bringing him out crashed into the Naga Hills.
Author's collection

resupply was unique. In his plan, pack animals would carry initial supplies but thereafter RAF aircraft would drop supplies by parachute to the troops below, homed in by wireless and finally guided by smoke signals.

This proposal came at a time when military commanders in India were yearning for an offensive in Burma, after months of humiliating defeat. In July 1942 Wavell agreed to the creation of the LRPG, comprising about 3,000 men in the new 77th Indian Infantry Brigade. It was to consist of a mobile headquarters, a British battalion, a Gurkha battalion, two companies, rifle units, a signals section, a sabotage unit and a reconnaissance unit. It would operate in columns consisting of mixed personnel, some of whom would have first-hand knowledge of the terrain. One very unusual proposal was that each column should include an RAF officer with four RAF wireless operators. The RAF set they needed to carry was the standard Mark 1082/3 used in aircraft, which weighed over 200lb. This required specialist knowledge and had to be carried by a large artillery mule.

For the emblem of his brigade Wingate selected a mythological beast, the 'Chinthe', statues of which were to be found in many Burmese pagodas; it was part lion and part eagle, and thus represented both the ground and the airborne sides of his operations. The men who served in the brigade became known as Chindits, a name partly chosen since they would have to cross the Chindwin river on their expeditions. It was a name that would eventually achieve fame and admiration. A regiment, two companies and some other units were selected and sent to the Central Provinces of India, where they began training in jungle warfare.

This form of guerrilla action conformed with Winston Churchill's policy of attack in warfare. He also advocated a more ambitious operation by the entire Eastern Army. This was no less than a drive down the west coast of Burma and the recapture of Rangoon, following which the Japanese would be forced back into Siam. Although this was far too ambitious a project for the resources available, the man in charge of the operation would be Lieutenant-General N.M. Irwin, who had taken over command of the Eastern Army from Lieutenant-General Sir Charles Broad on 24 July 1942, while Lieutenant-General G.A.P. Scoones had assumed command of IV Corps.

Eventually a more limited operation was planned, involving a drive down the 90-mile long Mayu peninsula, in the north of Burma's Arakan district, followed by the recapture of Akyab Island. The 14th and 26th Indian Divisions were selected to carry out this task. These two divisions formed part of Slim's XV Corps, but he was told that Irwin would exercise direct operational control over them during this offensive. The timing was scheduled for the next dry season, which began in November 1942 and lasted to May 1943. This period was more favourable for health reasons. Leeches, scorpions and snakes were far less in evidence, but there was still malaria to cope with as well as ticks that carried scrub typhus.

Slim's task in the next few months was not to engage on this project but to concentrate on training three new divisions which joined his XV Corps at Ranchi. These were the 7th Indian Infantry Division commanded by Major-General Frank Messervy, which had not yet had operational experience, the 5th Indian Infantry Division commanded by Major-General H.R. Briggs, which had arrived from the conflict in the Middle East, and the new 20th Indian Infantry Division commanded by Major-General Douglas D. Gracey.

The expansion of the RAF in Bengal progressed slowly before the Arakan campaign began, although there was considerable success in the construction in Assam of forward airstrips and their attendant services. The Japanese Air Force in Burma had been built up to about 200 front-line aircraft, and these had concentrated on attacking the airfields in northern Assam from which the USAAF was flying supplies into China. On 26 October 1942 they switched to daylight and night raids on these newly built RAF airstrips further south around Chittagong, but not with their usual persistence.

It seemed that the Japanese were being careful to avoid losses while the Americans and Australians were beginning to make headway against their forces in the Pacific. By the time the campaign in the Arakan began, the RAF's 224 Group was able to provide, for close support of the troops and for defence of these forward airstrips, five squadrons of Hurricanes, one of Mohawks and three of Blenheims. There was also a single flight of Lysanders for liaison work.

The rainfall was unusually heavy in the first weeks of November 1942. The 47th, 55th, 88th and 123rd Brigades of the 14th Indian Division, commanded by Major-General W.L. Lloyd, began the Arakan campaign on 9 December when they left Cox's Bazaar on the coast of Assam and crossed the border into Burma. Then they split into two main groups, with one heading towards the west coast and the other south-east down both banks of the Mayu river. A single regiment and some irregular troops from 'V' Force advanced down the Kaladan Valley in the east, to protect the left flank of the main groups.

These initial marches were almost unopposed and by 16 December one group had reached the Burmese port of Maungdaw, where the estuary of the Naf river flowed into the Bay of Bengal; the other group reached the inland town of Buthidaung a day later. These two places were connected by the only road that ran east–west across the Mayu peninsula, passing through two tunnels. Thereafter the two groups of the 14th Indian Division were separated by the dense jungle of the central Mayu Range, up to 2,000ft in height, which ran down the whole peninsula and was considered by British troops to be almost impenetrable.

All seemed to go well in the next advances, with some troops left behind to protect rear communications. Intelligence from 'V' Force indicated that the Japanese had had time to build up their forces and to construct defences in the south of the peninsula. By the end of December the troops of the 14th Indian Division were at the port of Donbaik near the western tip of the Mayu peninsula, while the eastern group was approaching Rathedaung on the far side of the

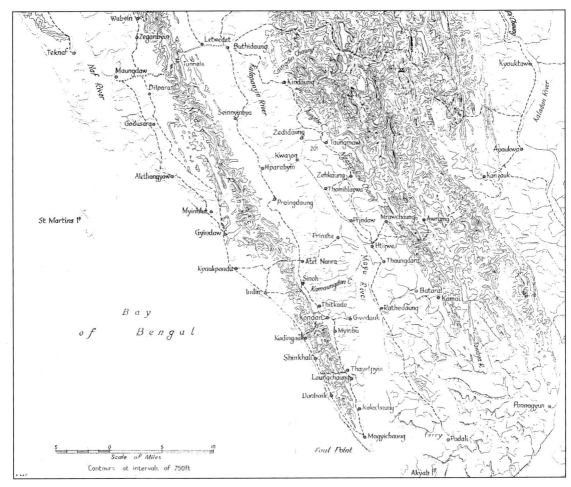

Area of combat in the Mayu Range of the Arakan, from the Maungdaw–Buthidaung road in the north to Akyab in the south, with the Kaladan river in the east.

Mayu river. Then both had to halt while supplies were brought up along the long and difficult route from railheads in Assam.

Meanwhile Lieutenant-General Iida, who still commanded the Japanese 15th Army in Burma, had ordered his 55th Division under Lieutenant-General Takishi Koga to cross to Akyab, while his troops in the tip of the Mayu peninsula were ordered to defend it at all costs. The Japanese movements were being harried by attacks from the RAF. However, their troops in the peninsula succeeded in constructing defence lines of very effective bunkers, made of heavy logs and covered with about five feet of earth, which were impervious to shellfire and very difficult to spot from the air. These were not only cleverly concealed but situated in such a way that each was protected by crossfire. Lloyd's frontal attacks against both Donbaik and Rathedaung were brought to a halt by these defences, with heavy losses.

Reinforcements were sent to Lloyd. The 6th British Brigade from the 2nd

80

British Division was allocated on 9 February 1943 to reinforce the front against Donbaik. The 4th British Brigade and the 23rd, 36th and 71st Indian Brigades from the 26th Indian Division followed later. On their arrival Lloyd had the unusually large number of nine brigades in his 14th Indian Division. He also asked for a force of Valentine tanks to be sent from Chittagong. Eight of these duly arrived but all were knocked out on their first attack on the bunkers at Donbaik. There were no vessels available for a seaborne outflanking attack on this defensive position, while the central Mayu Range was still considered impassable for troops. The last frontal attack on Donbaik took place on 19 March but once again was repulsed with more losses.

Then the Japanese began to counter-attack, despite their inferior numbers. A force of about three battalions, led by the resourceful and determined Colonel Tamahashi, approached from the east and scattered the flanking troops in the Kaladan Valley. Tamahashi then turned on the rear of the troops outside Rathedaung but these managed to break through the Japanese lines to retreat northwards in small parties.

Faced with problems on all fronts, Lloyd ordered the two brigades opposing Donbaik, the 47th Indian and the 6th British, to begin withdrawing northwards on 29 March. But the defeat of troops in the southern area of the Mayu river was not enough for Tamahashi. He sent his battalions with pack-guns across the Mayu Range, following narrow tracks through the jungle that the British had considered impenetrable. On the night of 5 April they descended on the rear of the 6th British Brigade retreating along the western coastal strip, killing a company commander and most of his staff. Very confused fighting followed but the British soldiers rallied and managed to hold off the Japanese in order to continue their retreat.

At the end of March Lieutenant-General Irwin had decided to take over temporary command of the 14th Indian Division from Lloyd. He then appointed Major-General C.E.N. Lomax, who at the time was in command of the 26th Indian Division, to take over this position when he was able to do so four days later. Lomax inherited a very confused situation, with the nine brigades scattered and disorganised.

Perhaps the most favourable aspect at this stage was the work being carried out by the RAF. The fighters of 224 Group, which by then had increased to nine squadrons equipped with Hurricanes and two with Mohawks, were harrying Tamahashi's troops remorselessly, making about 150 sorties a day from their forward airstrips in Assam. They had already flown numerous sorties during the campaign. The bombers of 221 Group were also extremely active, having been built up to one squadron equipped with Consolidated Liberators, one with Vickers Wellingtons and three with Bristol Blenheims. In addition, one of the former Blenheim squadrons had spent some weeks converting to Beaufighter VIs. Carrying up to 1,650lb of bombs and armed with four 20mm cannon in the nose plus six machine-guns in the wings, this aircraft was extremely deadly in the ground-attack role. The first operation had begun on 25 December 1942 and 27 Squadron's Beaufighters soon became loathed by the Japanese. It earned the nickname *Whispering Death* in this theatre of war, owing to its fairly silent and low-level approach coupled with enormous fire-power. In their attacks on enemy positions and supply routes, the aircraft of both 221 and 224 Groups were giving the Japanese a foretaste of their increasing effectiveness in Burma.

Lomax understood from 'V' Force that the Japanese intended to retake the Maungdaw–Buthidaung road. He disposed some of his forces south of this line, for the first time placing some of them in the jungle of the Mayu Range. Other forces were situated behind this line, giving defence in depth.

On 14 April the higher command of the 14th Division was passed to XV Corps and thus to Lieutenant-General Slim, while Lomax remained in operational command. Slim had taken no active part in the Arakan campaign, although he had visited the area twice to provide reports for Wavell. He then visited Lomax every few days and was impressed by his calm and skilful approach to the situation. In fact, the Japanese showed no inclination to attack the defence line he had set up, although there was always the possibility that they might try to hook round from the east.

Lieutenant-General Takishi Koga, commander of the 55th Division, 15th Army, during the Japanese counter-offensive in the Arakan, March–May 1943.

Author's collection

Lomax was not content with remaining on the defensive and planned to lure the Japanese into a trap by leaving open part of this defence line, but disposing his troops along three sides of a box, with a reserve to close on the Japanese from behind when they advanced. The Japanese duly obliged on 2 May, but Lomax's tactic did not work out as planned. Indeed, the ferocity of the Japanese attack broke the resolution of the defending troops, who seemed to be tired and demoralised after months of defeat.

This development signalled the end of any offensive action by the 14th Indian Division in this Arakan campaign. Lomax received reports from 'V' Force of Japanese movements circling round from the east. It was time to arrange as orderly a retreat as possible. The ferries at Buthidaung were destroyed and the troops moved out on the night of 6/7 May. Maungdaw was evacuated on 11 May and the battle-weary troops made their way back to Chittagong, from where they had started out the previous December. Lieutenant-General Koga took up defensive positions on the Maungdaw–Buthidaung line before the monsoon put a stop to any further advances by his Japanese troops.

This operation had cost the 14th Indian Division about 2,500 men killed, wounded and missing, for no gain at all. A far greater number of those who returned were suffering from malaria. Morale slumped, not only among the humiliated survivors but among those troops who had not participated in the conflict. The Japanese had confirmed their superiority as invincible fighters, able to overcome forces far greater than their own number. Yet something had already happened which helped to change this belief among the British and Indian troops.

The first Chindit expedition was originally intended to coincide with an assault on northern Burma by the Chinese troops gathered in Yunnan. When the latter proved premature, Wingate argued that his expedition should go ahead in any event, partly because his men were fully trained and keyed up, partly to demonstrate that such an expedition was possible, and partly to provide an example of British and Indian troops 'beating the Japanese at their own game' with the benefit of new tactics.

Eventually Wavell agreed and 31 Squadron, equipped with Dakotas and commanded by Wing Commander W.H.H. Burbury, moved to Agartala in East Bengal. The airborne supplies were stored on the airfield ready to be dropped, in the words of Wingate, 'Like Father Christmas, down the chimney.' The expedition marched out of Assam, the region held by IV Corps, on 8 February 1943. Of the seven columns, three were British, with each consisting of 306 men, while four were Gurkha, with each consisting of 369 men. The columns were numbered 1 to 8, no. 6 having been merged with the others. Each column was provided with fifteen horses and a hundred mules. In addition, each man carried a pack weighing 70lb. Their armament included rifles, anti-tank rifles, machine-guns and 3-inch mortars. They also carried dynamite.

Two of the Gurkha columns formed a Southern Group, mainly to provide an initial diversionary force, while the other five formed a Northern Group. The Southern Group, consisting of nos 1 and 2 Gurkha columns, crossed the Chindwin river on the nights of 14/15 and 15/16 February 1943, about 50 miles to the south of the Northern Group. The 23rd Division of IV Corps had already sent two battalions towards Kalewa in Burma to collaborate with this part of the operation. To help further with the deception plan, Major J.H. Jeffries of the 142nd Commando Company accompanying the two Chindit columns was required to wear the badges of a brigadier in the locations through which they passed. It was hoped that the Japanese would believe a whole brigade was on the march.

The Northern Group, together with Wingate's headquarters, began to cross the Chindwin river during daylight on 14 February 1943. The objectives of both groups were to cut the main railway line between Mandalay and Myitkyina, to harass the Japanese in the Shwebo area and if possible to cross the Irrawaddy and cut the railway between Mandalay and Lashio.

The air drops were achieved as planned in the early part of the operation. It was at first arranged for these to be made over open country such as paddy fields

Chindits wading through a shallow stream on their outward journey to cut the Mandalay–Myitkyina railway on their first expedition. All boats and rafts were burnt before they continued.

Author's collection

The mythological Chinthe, part lion and part eagle, which was adopted by the Chindits as their emblem. This bronze example is one of a pair brought to England before the war by Laurence Kirk, an official on the oilfields of the Yenangyaung.

Jane Kirk collection

but with practice it proved possible for the airmen to pick out the smoke signals of columns and home in on small jungle clearings.

The Southern Group was the first to encounter serious trouble. No. 1 Column destroyed a bridge on the Mandalay–Myitkyina railway on 2 March, but No. 2 Column was ambushed and scattered. Some of the survivors made their way back to Assam but others joined up with No. 1 Column, which continued eastwards to the Irrawaddy, which it crossed on 10 March.

The five columns of Northern Group reached a position about 35 miles east of the Mandalay–Myitkyina railway on 1 March and went into bivouac. Wingate ordered three columns to move south and create a diversion while the other two pressed on to the railway line. One of these three diversionary columns, No. 4, clashed with the enemy on 4 March and lost men, mules and equipment, including its wireless. The commander decided that the survivors should make their way back to Assam. The other two columns, Nos 7 and 8, carried on their diversions and headed eastwards for the Irrawaddy. After avoiding some Japanese positions they crossed the river successfully on 18 March.

Wingate had ordered the other two columns in the Northern Group, Nos 3 and 5, to advance to the railway line and begin the destruction. They did so most effectively, cutting it in over seventy places. In some instances thousands of tons of rock from gorges were blasted down over the track. Then both columns headed eastwards on their separate routes to the Irrawaddy. No. 5 Column crossed this successfully on the night of 10/11 March but No. 3 had some fiercely fought encounters with the Japanese, losing most of its mules and equipment. The survivors crossed the river on 13 March, after which they joined up with No. 5 Column.

Wingate and his headquarters staff had crossed the Irrawaddy on 17 March. He contemplated further action with the aid of some enthusiastic Kachin tribesmen who wished to get rid of Japanese rule. This did not seem feasible with the forces and equipment available, and in any event on 24 March he was ordered by IV Corps to withdraw. One major reason for this was the problem of airborne supply at a greater distance, not so much for the Dakotas but for the fighter aircraft ensuring their safety. All the five remaining Chindit columns retreated, breaking up into smaller parties and then undergoing extraordinary experiences.

According to official figures, 2,182 men returned from about 3,000 who participated in the operation. These men had marched for at least 750 miles and some for much more, having penetrated about 200 miles behind enemy lines. The role of the RAF was acclaimed as extremely successful during the mission, although there were some mishaps. The Dakotas flew 178 sorties, of which only 19 were unsuccessful, and dropped a total of 300 tons of supplies to the columns. Some of the early drops were not collected by the ground troops but accuracy improved steadily with experience. Usually several runs had to be made over the target, with the dispatchers kicking out about seven packages on each run, so

The Vultee Vengeance was a two-seat dive-bomber which served with the RAF only in the Burma theatre. It was armed with four machine-guns in the wings and two more in the rear cockpit, and also carried 2,000lb of bombs. Four squadrons of the RAF and three squadrons of the Indian Air Force were equipped with the Vengeance from August 1942 onwards. They carried out very effective attacks against Japanese targets, which were difficult to spot in the jungle.

Author's collection

Stationary wagons on the railway line between Mandalay on the Irrawaddy river and Monywa on the Chindwin river under attack on 18 July 1943 with cannon and machine-guns by Beaufighter VIs of 27 Squadron based at Agartala in India. The area was agricultural, supplying food for the Japanese forces as well as cotton.

Author's collection

that all descended within a small area for collection. One of the most dramatic flights took place on 28 April when Flying Officer Vlasto managed to land his Dakota in a small clearing and then take off again with seventeen sick and wounded men from a returning party.

Although this first Chindit operation cannot be counted as a military success in terms of the effort involved and the losses incurred, it certainly had an electrifying effect on the general public in Britain and even in the USA. Cleverly handled with headline news and photographs, the publicity of this unusual exploit provided the first good news concerning Burma to reach those at home. It had a very dramatic quality that appealed to the British character. The Americans were also impressed with the story and began to form their own LRPG in the Burma theatre, consisting of about 3,000 volunteers. This was named the 5307th Composite Unit (Provisional) and was commanded by Colonel F.D. Merrill, Stilwell's Chief of Staff. It later became known as Merrill's Marauders.

The news also helped to hearten the Allied troops who so far had experienced, or heard about, nothing but defeat in the war against the Japanese in Burma. Perhaps even more importantly, it inaugurated a new method of warfare particularly suited to the conditions of the Burmese terrain: the close collaboration of the RAF with ground troops as a means of supply. In the words of Wingate, 'A weapon has been found which may well prove a counter to the obstinate but unimaginative qualities of the Japanese soldier and which will give scope to the military qualities which the British soldier still shares with his ancestors.'

The Japanese seemed at first to have been somewhat mystified about this expedition, but before long they appreciated that the whole of northern Burma was vulnerable to such infiltration. Lieutenant-General R. Mutaguchi, who had taken over command of the 15th Army from Lieutenant-General Koga, decided that the best method of putting a stop to further incursions would be to invade and occupy eastern Assam in the next dry season. He came under the authority of Lieutenant-General M. Kawabe, who had been appointed Commander of the new Burma Army Headquarters formed on 27 March 1943. This plan contravened the previous policy of remaining on defence along the border with India. Moreover, it made no provision for the airborne supply of Japanese troops in their advance.

In April 1943 the Japanese parachuted a number of agents into Assam, disaffected Indians who sought the complete independence of their country from Britain. All these were soon captured and two were 'turned' to become double agents. One of them was codenamed *Owl* and he proved very useful for Fleming's GSI (d) section of the Military Intelligence Directorate. He was fed at first with low-grade but correct military intelligence, of little value to the Japanese but enough to gain their confidence in its reliability. Thereafter he was constantly supplied with misinformation, and this was given credence by the Japanese.

American sappers trying to find a shorter route for a section of the Ledo Road in the Naga jungle. This road was under construction from Ledo in Assam through northern Burma and then across the Hukaung Valley to Chungking in China. Its purpose was to supply war materials to the forces in both Burma and China. Work was begun, cutting through precipitous hills and through uncharted jungles. It involved enormous effort, but in the event most of the supplies were carried by air.

Author's collection

There was a change in the Allied Command on 26 May 1943 when General Sir George Gifford took over command of the Eastern Army from Lieutenant-General Irwin. Similarly, on 20 June General Sir Claude Auchinleck succeeded Field Marshal Sir Archibald Wavell as Commander-in-Chief in India.

Major events in other theatres of war had moved in favour of the Allies by this time. Australian troops had been largely responsible for the first decisive defeat of Japanese troops, having crushed them in New Guinea during a campaign ending in December 1942, in jungle conditions similar to those in Burma. The German Sixth Army had been wiped out by the Russians on the outskirts of Stalingrad in the same month. Following the retreat of the German Afrika Korps in the Western Desert and then the Allied invasion of North-West Africa in operation 'Torch' of November 1942, the Axis forces had been cleared out of Africa by May 1943. Italy was tottering on the brink of defeat.

By July 1943 both the RAF and the USAAF in India were being built up to formidable numbers of squadrons equipped with modern aircraft. Progress was being made with improving the road and rail transport systems in eastern Bengal and Assam. Another great endeavour, the construction of a road from Ledo over the mountains to a point on the old Burma Road beyond Japanese lines, was under way by American experts with their modern bulldozers. The Allies were eager to take more offensive action in Burma. Plans were afoot for another campaign in the Arakan, a seaborne invasion of the Andaman Islands, an advance from Imphal towards Indaw to coincide with another from Yunnan, and yet another from Ledo down to Myitkyina. In the event these did not turn out exactly as anticipated.

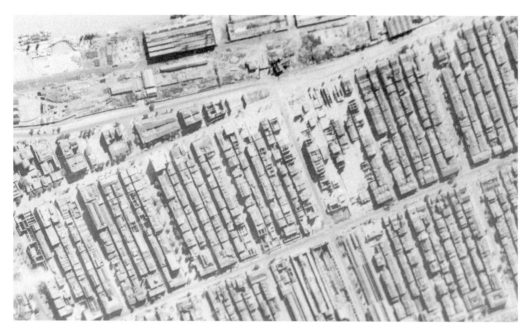

The docks at Rangoon in the south of Burma, off the Gulf of Martaban, photographed in 1943 by an RAF reconnaissance aircraft, probably from Dum-Dum in Bengal.

Squadron Leader J.D. Braithwaite collection

Students from all parts of India underwent a special course in the Poona Engineering College to qualify as Air Mechanics in the Indian Air Force. The latter was tiny in 1941 but by 1944 had expanded to five squadrons of Hurricanes and Vengeances. These trainees are learning how to fit a Gipsy aero engine.

Author's collection

Armoured carriers manufactured in an Indian railway workshop ready for transport to the campaign in Burma.

Author's collection

An assembly line of Bren carriers in an Australian railway workshop, destined for the war in South-East Asia and the South Pacific.

Author's collection

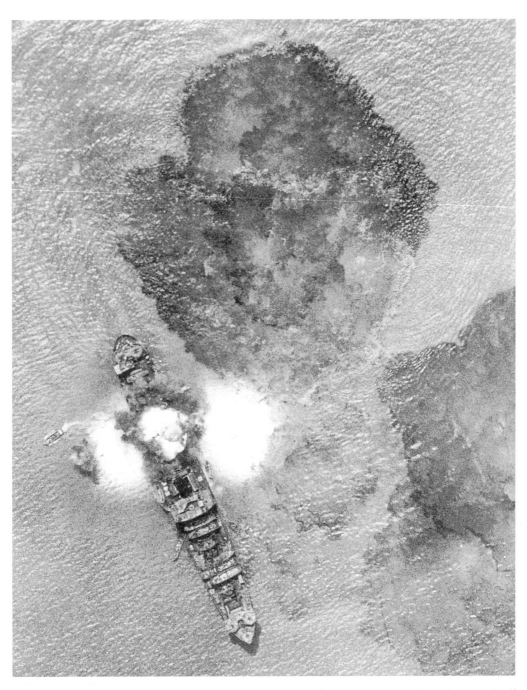

The Japanese merchant vessel *Asakasan Maru* of 8,709 tons being bombed from low level off Moulmein in south-east Burma on 27 February 1943 by B-24 Liberators of the 10th USAAF in India commanded by Major-General L.H. Brereton. Lifeboats can be seen rescuing the crew before the vessel sank.

Author's collection

The main airfield at Toungoo, near the Sittang river about 125 miles north of Rangoon, was photographed in early 1943 by an RAF reconnaissance aircraft. The airfield had been developed for use by the Japanese Air Force.

Squadron Leader J.D. Braithwaite collection

Lieutenant-General N.S.M. Irwin (left), who took command of India's Eastern Army on 24 July 1942, pictured with Major-General W.L. Lloyd, commander of the 14th Indian Division.

Author's collection

An animal barge employed by the Allied forces on the Naf river, on the border of north Arakan with south Bengal.

Author's collection

A view in the north of the Arakan, looking south-west from the town of Buthidaung, over the valley of the Mayu river (known as the Kalapanzin river in these upper reaches) towards the steep, jungle-clad hills of the Mayu Range.

Author's collection

Some idea of the conditions endured by troops in the Burma campaign is given by this photograph of a patrol of the Yorks and Lancs Regiment making its way up a hillside covered with dense elephant grass. The men had to endure sweltering heat, vermin and the possibility of fever, in addition to combat with a fanatical enemy.

Author's collection

A smoke bomb set off by the Chindits in their first expedition. The supply-dropping Dakotas were directed towards their targets by RAF wireless operators accompanying the Chindit columns. However, the precise positions in the jungle needed to be indicated since it was almost impossible to spot them from above.

Author's collection

In March 1943 one of the Chindit columns sent an SOS to base with information that it was short of food and ammunition, and that seventeen men were sick or wounded. The column was located and supplies were dropped, but the RAF Dakota could not land. The Chindits then laid out a landing strip and arranged parachutes to spell out the words PLANE LAND HERE NOW.

Author's collection

A few days after the first supply drop, an RAF Dakota landed safely on the prepared strip. This photograph shows supplies being dragged away with all possible speed. The Dakota then took off with the seventeen sick and wounded on board.

Author's collection

(*Above*) Two of the men from the Chindit column looking cheerful in the Dakota during their flight to safety. Left to right: Lance Sergeant Leslie Flowers and Private William Crowhurst.

Author's collection

(*Opposite*) Here an RAF dispatcher in the Dakota is handing a can of water to a Chindit suffering from dysentery and an infected hip. The Chindit is holding on to the static line used for parachute hooks.

Author's collection

Two Chindits, looking happy after their safe return. All the survivors had marched at least 750 miles and most covered 1,000 miles, during a period of ten to twelve weeks.

Author's collection

CHAPTER FOUR

The Crucial Battles

The Allied command structure in the Burma theatre underwent a major change in the late summer of 1943. It had been decided by leaders of the Western Powers at a conference codenamed 'Trident', held in Washington during the previous May, that there should be a unified command. This became effective in another conference codenamed 'Quadrant' held during August in Quebec, when Admiral Lord Louis Mountbatten was appointed Supreme Commander of the new South-East Asia Command (SEAC). He arrived in India in the following month to begin work on his new duties.

At the age of 43, Lord Louis Mountbatten was relatively young to hold such a major position. Nevertheless he had had over twenty-five years' experience in the Royal Navy. Perhaps more importantly for his selection, he had been Chief of Combined Operations for the previous two years, which included the Anglo-American invasion of Northwest Africa in October 1942 under the codename 'Torch'. He was known to be ambitious and to possess boundless energy.

The area of the new SEAC included the whole of India, Ceylon, Burma, Malaya, Sumatra, Siam and French Indo-China. Lieutenant-General Joseph Stilwell was appointed as Deputy Supreme Commander of SEAC, in addition to his existing functions as Chief of Staff to Generalissimo Chiang Kai-Shek and commander of the Chinese forces operating from India. The appointment mollified this acerbic but respected American commander and stressed the Anglo-American nature of SEAC.

The naval forces of SEAC, known as the Eastern Fleet, were commanded by Admiral Sir James Somerville. By mid-November 1943 his forces in the Indian Ocean consisted of one battleship, one aircraft carrier, seven cruisers, two armed merchant vessels, eleven destroyers, thirteen escort vessels and six submarines. It had been hoped that major amphibious operations would be possible against Japanese forces in Burma, Malaya and Sumatra, but these proved impossible since suitable landing craft could not be provided. All these were still needed in the European theatre for operations against German forces in Italy after that country had surrendered on 8 September 1943, as well as for the forthcoming invasions of Normandy and Southern France.

The British and Indian Army formations in SEAC came under the new Eleventh Army Group commanded by General Sir George Giffard. Within this was the new Fourteenth Army commanded by Lieutenant-General William Slim, which included his old XV Corps with headquarters near Cox's Bazaar as well as IV Corps with headquarters in Imphal. Each of these two corps consisted of three divisions but there were two more in reserve. This Fourteenth Army was in fact the previous Eastern Command, under a new name but better equipped and trained. The legendary Phoenix bird, which rose from its own ashes, was taken as the symbol of this resurgent force.

Also within the Eleventh Army Group a single division and a brigade formed the Ceylon Army Command. Apart from this there was the new XXXIII Corps with five divisions and a tank brigade under training, plus six Long Range Penetration (LRP) brigades also under training. Distinct from the Eleventh Army Group was the new Northern Combat Area Command (NCAC) under Stilwell. This consisted of three Chinese divisions, plus the 5307th Composite Unit (Merrill's Marauders) under training.

The new Air Command of SEAC was not formed until 12 December 1943. Its headquarters in New Delhi were commanded by Air Chief Marshal Sir Richard Peirse, but subordinate to this was a new Eastern Air Command under the command of Major-General George E. Stratemeyer of the USAAF. By comparison with the air forces available in 1942, this was an enormous and hard-hitting organisation. Its 3rd Tactical Air Force under Air Marshal Sir John Baldwin consisted of 221 Group at Comilla with nine RAF fighter squadrons, plus 224 Group at Chittagong with sixteen RAF fighter or fighter-bomber squadrons. Then there was the Northern Air Sector Force at Dinjan under Colonel J.F. Egan of the USAAF, consisting of seven USAAF and three RAF fighter squadrons. The Strategic Air Force at Calcutta under Brigadier-General H.C. Davidson consisted of seven USAAF and three RAF long-range bomber squadrons. The Troop Carrier Command at Calcutta under Brigadier-General W.D. Old of the USAAF consisted of two USAAF and three RAF squadrons equipped with Dakotas, plus another RAF squadron with Hudsons. Lastly the Photographic Reconnaissance Force at Comilla under Group Captain S.G. Wise consisted of three USAAF and two RAF squadrons.

There were even more squadrons in this new Air Command, South-East Asia, coming directly under the control of its headquarters. There were ten fighter and bomber squadrons based in Ceylon within the RAF's 222 Group commanded by Air Vice-Marshal A. Lees, and three more in the RAF's 225 Group at Bangalore commanded by Air Commodore P.H. Mackworth. Finally, there were six fighter and bomber squadrons of the USAAF and fourteen more of the RAF and the RIAF undergoing training and not yet committed to operational roles.

Mountbatten had discussed the air-to-ground supply system with Wingate at the Washington conference and was convinced that it represented the key to success in the war against the Japanese in his area. However, there was a small but vital problem that needed to be overcome. There was a dearth of parachutes in India for the operations that lay ahead. Mountbatten sent a request to England

Admiral Lord Louis Mountbatten (Supreme Allied Commander of South-East Asia Command from 16 November 1943 to 31 May 1946) with Lieutenant-General R.A. Wheeler of the US Army (Principal Administrative Officer from 16 November 1943 to 23 September 1945).

Author's collection

for 500 sewing machines to help increase production but there remained the difficulty of obtaining supplies of silk from which canopies and rigging lines were normally made. The parachutes contained in seat-packs and chest-packs carried by aircrew, opened by ripcords, were in huge demand elsewhere for the increasing numbers of RAF and USAAF squadrons. Together with the harnesses worn by aircrew in flight, each pack cost about £70. The parachutes used for dropping supplies were far simpler but each cost about £20.

Fortunately this problem was solved by Slim and his headquarters team, in cooperation with manufacturers in Calcutta. This was the world centre for paper mills employing the natural fibre jute. Within ten days of a request, the manufacturers of the mills had devised a woven cloth and a cord from which a suitably sized canopy and rigging lines could be made of jute. The result was shown to deliver a supply package safely from air to ground. Moreover, each parachute cost only £1. Before long, these new 'parajutes' were streaming out of the paper mills in Calcutta.

Mountbatten determined to change the character of warfare in Burma by continuing to campaign throughout the year instead of solely in the dry season. This posed a serious challenge to the health of the troops on the ground during the monsoon period. For every battle casualty in 1942/3 there had been 120 who had fallen sick with malaria, scrub-typhus, dysentery or other ailments. A new Medical Advisory Division managed to obtain huge supplies of DDT insecticide spray for use in the pestilent areas, while troops were provided with a daily dose of mepacrine, a synthetic substitute for quinine, used to combat malaria. The sickness rate began to fall dramatically, eventually reducing the proportion to six falling sick to one battle casualty.

Another major problem was the inadequate road and rail supply system to the ground forces in the front lines within the eastern states of Assam and Manipur. Improvements had begun in March 1942 when volunteer labour detachments had been sent to improve the highways, to make a start on the new Ledo Road, and to lay new oil pipelines. The railways remained inadequate, with some broad-gauge lines while others were metre or 2 ft 6 in gauge. Mountbatten decided to put 800 miles of track under military control and made arrangements for US Railway Battalions to start work on them. About 4,000 men arrived, improving the quality of the lines and converting the narrow gauge to metre. The volume of traffic began gradually to increase from 90,000 tons monthly to 200,000 tons monthly.

Morale among the troops was another great concern to Mountbatten. Although this was improving with the events of recent months, more needed to be done. He embarked on a series of visits to troops and airmen in the front lines. His normal method was to stand on an ammunition box or a packing case and address all ranks crowded in front of him. He usually began by saying, 'I understand you believe you're the forgotten army. That's not true.' Then, when the men had resigned themselves to the usual pep talk, he continued, 'The truth is nobody's ever bloody well heard of you!' All the men burst into laughter and he had their eager attention. He went on to describe how there would be no retreat in future, supremacy over the Japanese Air Force was being achieved, their supplies could come from the air, new SEAC newspapers would be delivered to them daily, casualties would be evacuated to well-equipped hospitals in India and even that, unlike the Japanese, they would be able to fight throughout the monsoon. He dismissed the belief that the Japanese soldier was a superman, describing him as an ignoramus who had been indoctrinated to believe that his emperor was a god. He stressed that intelligent free men could 'whip him every time'.

Most of Mountbatten's measures were extensions of moves that had been taking place before his arrival, but he brought a new impetus to them when additional resources were becoming available. At the same time the Japanese had changed their views on this theatre of war. They had experienced a series of serious reverses following counter-attacks by the Americans and Australians in the Pacific. Their commanders contrasted these with their unbroken string of successes in Malaya and Burma, against what seemed to be a weaker enemy. If they could continue to the conquest of India, supplies to China would cease and the long war in that country would be won. Increased military force and huge additional supplies could then be brought to bear in the Pacific. Thus they planned a so-called 'March on Delhi'.

Towards the end of 1943 Allied Intelligence learnt that more Japanese forces were entering Burma. Four Japanese divisions had faced them during that year, together with an air division based in Rangoon. However, it became known that three more divisions were moving into Burma, one from Java, another from Siam and another from Malaya. These movements accorded with the Allied policy of drawing Japanese forces away from the Pacific theatre, but the army commanders in India realised that they now faced a more powerful enemy. Moreover the Japanese divisions were augmented by contingents of their 'Indian National Army', recruited by the nationalist Chandra Bose in Singapore from Indian civilians and former army personnel. Although the fighting quality of these men was not considered high, their presence indicated that the Japanese intended to advance into India and encourage the population to rise against British rule.

It was SEAC which made the first move in the forthcoming battles. This was again in the Arakan, which had become known as the Southern Front, but the immediate objective was somewhat limited. In the absence of landing craft that could operate down the west coast, it was decided to advance overland and retake the small port of Maungdaw on the estuary of the Naf river, so that some supplies for any further advances could be brought in by merchant vessels from Calcutta. As early as mid-November 1943 XV Corps of Slim's Fourteenth Army had been assembling for this task, under the command of Lieutenant-General A.P.F. Christison.

The Japanese had reinforced the Maungdaw–Buthidaung road with underground constructions in the two tunnels which passed through the Mayu Range, by burrowing deep within them a labyrinth of storerooms and barracks. The four entrances of the tunnels were heavily defended while other fortified positions were sited in the range of jungle-clad hillocks along the 16-mile road, covering one another with crossfire. Two major positions were located in the west of Razabil, about 3 miles from Maungdaw, and in the east at Letwedet, about 3 miles from Buthidaung in the Mayu Valley.

Two Japanese divisions, the 54th and the 55th, were situated in the Arakan area, although some of their regiments were still approaching. Their overall commander was Lieutenant-General T. Hanaya of the 55th, whose 143rd Regiment was manning the front line. This was not only a defensive position but was intended as a starting point for one of the Japanese invasion routes into India. It would be very difficult to overcome but the Allies were far better equipped and organised than on the previous campaign.

Three divisions of XV Corps were detailed to make the advance. These were the 5th Indian Division under Major-General H.R. Briggs, down the Mayu Range

The winding road across the Mayu Range from Maungdaw to Buthidaung, photographed by the RAF towards the south over a stretch where it ran north–south. An entry to the west tunnel is in the foreground.

Author's collection

and the western coastal plain, the 7th Indian Division under Major-General F.R. Messervy, down both banks of the Kalapanzin (Mayu) river in the east, and the 81st West African Division under Major-General C.G. Woolner, down the Kaladan Valley further east, thus providing protection on the flank.

Before these advances began in the Arakan, some major improvements in communications had to be made, for Slim was determined that the main thrust down the Mayu peninsula should be accompanied by tanks, while the West Africans on the east flank should have the benefit of airborne supplies and airstrips. About 5 miles north of the Maungdaw–Buthidaung road was a narrow and winding footpath running east–west across the hills of the peninsula, via the Ngakydauk Pass. It seemed impossible to widen this for heavy vehicles but the 7th Divisional Engineers set about the task with the aid of a few bull-dozers. The path was first converted into a jeep track and then into a road capable of taking artillery and tanks. The pass itself, unpronounceable to British soldiers, became known as 'Okeydokey Pass'.

On the eastern flank in the Kaladan Valley the West Africans hacked out a jeep track some 70 miles long leading to their positions, and then cleared spaces in the jungle to form airstrips. It was not possible to bring tanks to them, but they would be the first division to be supplied entirely from the air. They were opposed by a single Japanese regiment plus some other units.

These preparations could not be concealed from the Japanese, who had also carried out an air reconnaissance of Calcutta and detected a build-up of shipping which could be used to supply the forward troops. On 5 December 1943 they mounted two major air attacks against about sixty vessels in the docks. The bombers were strongly escorted by fighters and the RAF Hurricanes defending the port fared badly against the 'Zeros', losing eight of their number. The bombers damaged three merchant vessels, a naval vessel, fifteen barges and many dock installations. They also caused 500 civilian casualties and many of the other Indian dock workers fled from the area.

Christison's XV Corps had begun advancing at the end of November, mopping up Japanese outposts and eventually reaching the main defence line. A huge offensive began on New Year's Eve when the 5th Indian Division opened an intense artillery bombardment of the Japanese positions at Razabil. At the same time the RAF's fighter-bombers blasted the Japanese positions, with the new Vultee Vengeance aircraft being guided in by artillery smoke shells. Then Lee-Grant medium tanks rumbled forward, with the infantry close behind them. The Japanese fought desperately and there were many casualties on both sides, but the defenders were so well dug-in that a few still held out. Meanwhile some of the attackers bypassed these defences and entered Maungdaw on 9 January 1944, to find it a shell of burnt-out buildings and wrecked docks. Nevertheless, the Divisional Engineers managed to clear the port of mines and to prepare a couple of berths for supply vessels. Before Razabil was completely overcome, Christison ordered most of his tanks eastwards over the 'Okeydokey' Pass to join in an attack by the 7th Division on the fortress at Letwedet near Buthidaung.

Although some form of Japanese counter-attack had been anticipated, it came as a complete surprise. On the night of 3/4 February it arrived from the unexpected direction of the *north* against a headquarters position of the 7th Division.

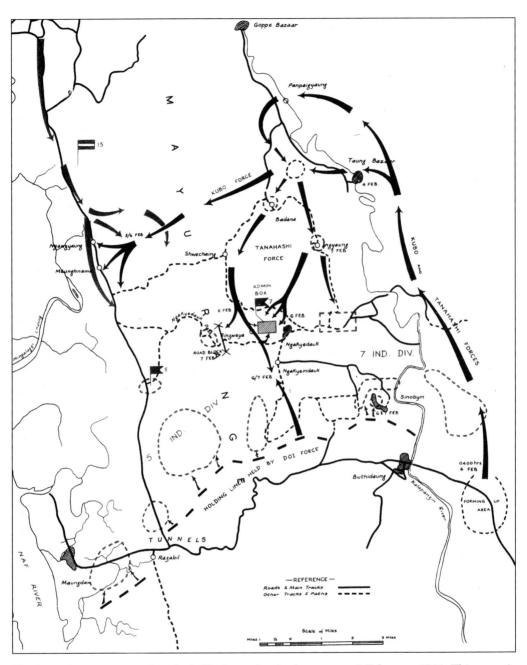

The Japanese attempt to invade India from the Arakan, as on 5 February 1944. This map is copied from the *Report to the Combined Chiefs of Staff by the Supreme Commander South-East Asia 1943–1945*, published by HMSO in 1951.

Unknown to XV Corps, the Japanese High Command had organised operation 'Ha-Go'. Its 55th Division in the Arakan had been split into three task forces under the overall command of Lieutenant-General Seizo Sakurai. The leading force, commanded by the formidable Colonel Tanahashi, moved up the eastern bank of the Mayu river and swept round the rear of the 7th Indian Division, cutting it off at 'Okeydokey' Pass. A smaller task force accompanied this but then swept around further west to the rear of the 5th Indian Division and cut off its supply route. The third task force began a general attack northwards from its positions in the Maungdaw–Buthidaung line.

About 8,000 fanatical Japanese took part in this operation, intended as a preliminary to their 'March on Delhi'. They were so sure of annihilating the two Indian divisions that they relied on capturing rations, transport and artillery to continue their advance. Their first blow fell on the rear administrative base of the 7th Indian Division, which had been set up at Sinzweya to the east of 'Okeydokey' Pass. It was preceded by screaming from the refugees who were being driven forward to cover the Japanese as they closed in. Messervy acted coolly and brought his forces into a more compact form, with clerks, orderlies and signalmen joining in the defences of the 'Admin Box', as it was called. Much of this fighting was hand-to-hand.

The situation became critical but not incapable of resolution. Slim ordered the 26th Indian Division to advance immediately from Chittagong to reinforce their comrades. Above all, there was no retreat from the Arakan. The 'Admin Box' was approximately a mile square and the troops of the 7th Indian Division defended it effectively, mostly over flat ground consisting of paddy fields. They had about two days' worth of rations at the outset but were told to stand firm while supplies poured in from the air. At the same time other supplies were dropped to the beleaguered 5th and 26th Indian Divisions advancing from the north to their support. The 81st West African Division in the Kaladan Valley also continued to receive supplies. These packages contained not only food and ammunition but anything requested by the troops on the ground. Instruments, spare parts for tanks and guns, clothing, cooking pans, drugs and plasma for the doctors, SEAC newspapers, mail for the soldiers – everything came from the sky. It put immense strain on the Dakota squadrons but their support was rated as magnificent. Some of the wounded were flown out by L-5 light aircraft while others were moved to an airstrip and successfully picked up by the Dakotas.

Japanese aircraft came over in increased numbers, but they received an unpleasant shock. Three RAF squadrons had been equipped with Spitfire VCs. With a Merlin 45 engine of 1,440hp, this fighter had a rapid rate of climb and a ceiling of 37,000ft. Armed with two 20mm cannon and four .303-inch machine-guns, it was more than a match for the Japanese 'Zero'. The troops on the ground were treated to the spectacle of Japanese aircraft streaming smoke and spiralling out of the sky to explode on impact in the jungle. It was estimated that during the first thirteen days of the battle these Spitfires probably destroyed or damaged

A mule train fording a river on the Arakan front, carrying supplies to the 7th Indian Division, Fourteenth Army, in February 1944.

Author's collection

Parachutes and containers falling from RAF Dakotas to troops of the 81st West African Division commanded by Major-General C.G. Woolner, during their advance down the Kaladan Valley in the second Arakan campaign.
Author's collection

Two men of the 7th Indian Division in the 'Admin Box', Private John Bache of Wellington in Somerset and Sergeant W. Meadows of Middlesbrough in Yorkshire, retrieving air-dropped supplies. About 1,540 tons were dropped to the troops in the eleven days they were surrounded by the Japanese.

Author's collection

sixty-five enemy aircraft for the loss of three of their own number. The Japanese lost control of the air. RAF Dakotas continued to supply the troops on the ground while bombers and fighter-bombers harried Japanese supply lines.

A further reinforcement, the 36th Indian Division commanded by Major-General F.W. Festing, left Chittagong but progress was slow over the difficult and lengthy roads. The main battle continued around the 'Admin Box', encircled by the Japanese in the surrounding hills, but the newly arrived 26th Indian Division began to harass the rear of their 55th Division. One night a group of Japanese managed to penetrate the defences of the 'Admin Box' and reach the Main Dressing Station. They slaughtered the wounded, the doctors and the orderlies, apart from a few who managed to hide in the jungle and later reported on the circumstances. This vicious action stiffened the resolve of the British and Indians, who were successful in wiping out the Japanese group on the following day.

Lieutenant-General Sakurai had planned on defeating the two Indian divisions within ten days and capturing sufficient supplies for continuing his advance. This objective had not been achieved by mid-February, although he had brought up strong reinforcements. The Japanese had lost heavily and were running short of food and ammunition. In the front line Lieutenant-General Hanaya was forced to order a retreat. His forces broke up into small units and tried to make their way back through the jungle, but many were caught and destroyed. The whole of the Buthidaung area was in the hands of the 7th Indian Division by the end of March and the fortress of Razabil was finally taken by the 5th Indian Division on 6 April.

The full number of the casualties suffered by the Japanese in this Arakan campaign is not known. During February alone the Allies counted over 5,000 bodies, amounting to over two-thirds of the invading force. This figure does not include those undiscovered in the jungle or those killed in the preceding and subsequent months, nor their wounded. The Allied casualties in the Arakan are recorded as 7,951 battle casualties during the nine months from November 1943 to July 1944, but these include the many wounded who were brought to safety and care. Although it was not a major campaign by comparison with other events, Mountbatten commented that 'the battle of Arakan marked the turning point in our campaign in Burma'.

This area of combat was only a part of the Japanese plans for their 'March on Delhi'. A larger thrust was made in the Central Front, under the codename 'U-Go', against Imphal in Manipur and Kohima in Assam. They intended to cross the Chindwin river and then the hills of Manipur and its river. They banked on annihilating the Allied armies, seizing transport and supplies, capturing airfields, destroying the air supply route to China, and advancing further into the Indian subcontinent. Three divisions of the Japanese 15th Army under Lieutenant-General R. Mutaguchi were assigned to this task. These were the 31st under Lieutenant-General K. Sato, the 15th under Lieutenant-General M. Yamauchi, and the 33rd under Lieutenant-General G. Yanagida. There were also considerable numbers of the 'Indian National Army', known as 'Jiffs' by the British troops.

The Central Front was defended by IV Corps commanded by Lieutenant-General Geoffrey A.P. Scoones, part of Slim's Fourteenth Army. This also consisted of three divisions, two of which were in forward positions along the border with Burma. These were the 17th Indian Division under Major-General D.T. 'Punch' Cowan, which had borne much of the brunt of the Japanese attack on Burma during 1942, and the 20th Indian Division under Major-General Douglas D. Gracey. The third was the 23rd Indian Division under Major-General Ouvrey L. Roberts, in reserve around Imphal.

The Japanese thrust was anticipated by SEAC and even welcomed, for it was considered preferable for the Allied forces to fight and destroy the enemy in this area than to advance into Burma and fight on extended supply lines. Plenty of notice had been obtained of the Japanese dispositions and main intentions. Air reconnaissance seldom picked out Japanese troop movements, for these usually took place at night, but photographs were taken of camouflaged rafts on the east bank of the Chindwin and large herds of cattle in advanced positions, which presaged a Japanese advance. Other information of a similar nature came from 'V' Force. More detailed intelligence came from documents, maps and orders taken from the bodies of Japanese killed in patrol clashes or in raids against their headquarters, for the soldiers had the careless habit of carrying these.

Operation 'U-Go' began on 6 March 1944, about a month after operation 'Ha-Go' had been launched in the Arakan. Regiments of the Japanese 33rd Division began crossing the Chindwin in the south of the defence line and making attacks on forward positions of the veteran 17th Indian Division based at Tiddim. As already arranged, the latter began to retreat along the road northwards towards Imphal, the capital of Manipur on the river of the same name, 167 miles distant on a plain of about 3,500 feet in height. The troops were in good heart after having been briefed about the tactics. Supplies were dropped to them through the unflagging efforts of the RAF Dakota squadrons. The men set mines in their rear and blew up bridges. The Japanese employed their usual tactics of sending fast-moving detachments around their columns to form road blocks, but the retreating troops had learnt how to deal with these and they were wiped out.

The other Japanese advances were ominous. To the north of their 33rd Division, their 15th Division advanced on 12 March from the Kabaw Valley towards Tamu, and then moved westwards in eight separate columns. This area was defended by the 20th Indian Division, which also began a fighting retreat, sometimes with tank-on-tank battles, towards Imphal. One of these Japanese columns crossed the Manipur river in the south of the area and threatened to cut off the 17th Indian Division before it reached Imphal. By 1 April the 20th Indian Division was concentrated in defensive positions around Palel, about 25 miles south-east of Imphal.

Even further north, the Japanese 31st Division crossed both the Chindwin and Manipur rivers and headed towards Kohima in Assam, which was only lightly garrisoned. This small town, on a plain about 4,500 feet in height, guarded the approach to Dimapur on the vital railway from Bengal, the loss of which would have been disastrous to the Allies.

Rapid improvements to the dispositions and strength of the Allied defences in Manipur and Assam were required, one of which concerned the capacity of air supply. While the fighters and fighter-bombers of the RAF could be relied upon to dominate the skies over both Indian states, there were insufficient Dakotas to cope with this additional area of operations. On 13 March Slim explained this critical situation to Mountbatten, who acted immediately by ordering SEAC's

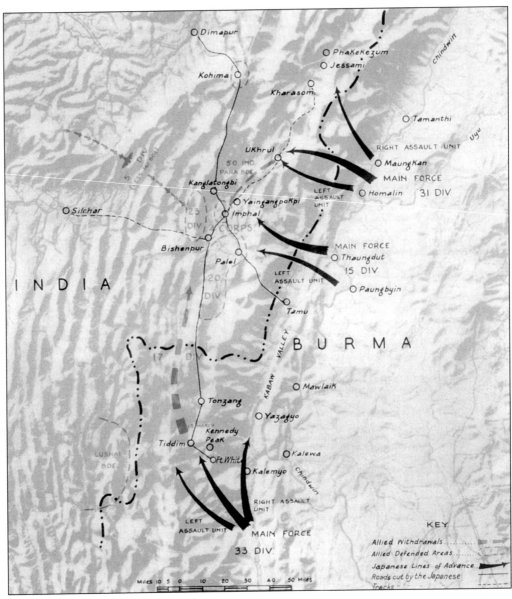

The Japanese attempt to invade Manipur and Assam, as on 15 March 1944. This map is copied from the *Report to the Combined Chiefs of Staff by the Supreme Commander South-East Asia 1943–1945*, published by HMSO in 1951.

Troop Carrier Command to divert thirty Dakotas from the 'Hump Run', without obtaining authority from the American Chiefs of Staff in Washington. Twenty of the larger Commando transports were provided, with a carrying capacity equivalent to thirty Dakotas. The Chiefs of Staff gave their approval later, partly since the air supply to China had increased enormously, from about 3,250 short tons in February 1943 to almost 14,500 tons in February 1944, so that a temporary reduction could be tolerated.

These Curtiss C-46 Commandos were employed along with Dakotas of the RAF's 194 Squadron in airlifting troops to the Central Front from the Arakan, where the battle had already been won. The fly-in began on 17 March with the 5th Indian Division commanded by Major-General H.R. Briggs. One of its brigades completed a transfer to the airfield at Imphal within three days, and was soon followed by a second brigade. The 7th Indian Division in the Arakan was warned that it would be required later.

Meanwhile, the knowledge that these reinforcements were due to arrive in Imphal enabled Scoones to order the dispatch of two brigades of the 23rd Indian

The Curtiss C-46 Commando of the USAAF shared the vital task of air supply with the Douglas C-47 Dakota, having a maximum take-off weight of 50,000lb compared with the Dakota's maximum take-off weight of 26,000lb. This photograph was taken over the Himalayas on the 'Hump Run', the route from Indian to Kunming in China, which was often beset by extremely dangerous weather conditions.

Author's collection

Division from the town, down the road towards the 17th Indian Division approaching along the road from Tiddim. Both converging divisions encountered strong Japanese forces about 70 miles from Imphal, including road blocks and tanks. Intense fighting took place, with the Allied divisions receiving close support from RAF fighter-bombers, and eventually the Japanese were routed. Patrols from the two Allied divisions met on 20 March and the 17th Division reached the area of Imphal on 5 April.

By far the most serious problem faced by Slim was the situation around Kohima. The potential loss of this little town was of no great importance except that its defences were more secure than those at Dimapur, where almost all the troops were staff members untrained in warfare. There was no airfield at Kohima, but its civilians and hospital cases were hastily evacuated by road to Dimapur and thence by rail further into India. The 161st Brigade of the 5th Indian Division from the Arakan was ordered to Dimapur, but far more reinforcements were urgently required. The 2nd British Division, part of XXXIII Corps under the command of Lieutenant-General Montague G.N. Stopford, was the most suitable but this was engaged on training in amphibious operations in the south of India and could be transported only by rail. Emergency measures on the Indian railways were made to facilitate its move and Stopford took over command in the Kohima area.

Meanwhile, Kohima was in peril. Its approaches were defended by a single battalion of mixed troops about 30 miles to the east but these faced the Japanese 31st Division of about 15,000 men. The Allied troops put up a tremendous resistance but were gradually forced back towards the town, where trenches and bunkers had been dug. Convalescents in the town had taken up arms to help with the defences but, even with these, the garrison numbered only about 1,000 men. The 161st Brigade completed its fly-in to Dimapur by the end of March. On 5 April it came to the relief of Kohima, but soon afterwards the town was completely invested by the Japanese. Meanwhile, the 2nd British Division under the command of Major-General John M.L. Grover was still in transit.

Fortunately the Japanese commander, Major-General K. Sato, did not appear to understand that he could have bypassed Kohima and taken Dimapur, or else he was simply obeying orders. The full weight of his attack continued to fall on Kohima. By this time the defenders had been forced back into an area of a rough square with sides no more than 1,000 yards long, and they were subjected to continuous mortar and artillery fire from the Japanese, who also cut off their water supply. A much smaller spring was found within the perimeter, very close to the Japanese positions, and collection at night was perilous. Rationing was introduced, with water confined to a pint a day for each man.

The RAF was continuously at work during this battle. The Dakotas had to drop their supplies from low level with pinpoint accuracy into a small area, and these included tyres filled with water as well as waterproof sheets in which to catch the rain. The fighter-bomber squadrons, equipped with Hurricanes and

An Allied tank moving northwards in April 1944 up the winding and precipitous road from Imphal to Kohima, in the vicinity of Ukhrul, while the battle for Kohima was still raging.

Author's collection

Vengeances, were particularly active. The Hurricane IIC, armed with four 20mm cannon and carrying two bombs of either 250lb or 500lb, was devastating against Japanese positions which were difficult to conceal from the air on the plains of Assam. Although less numerous than the Hurricanes, the Vengeance dive-bombers with six .30-inch guns and up to 2,000lb of bombs, were capable of an equivalent accuracy. Spitfires kept the skies clear of Japanese aircraft.

So the defenders held out for another fortnight, with their morale remaining surprisingly high while they inflicted heavy losses on their fanatical attackers. On 20 April the 2nd British Division from Dimapur completed its breakthrough and the original garrison was relieved. The exhausted men were able to march out, carrying their wounded, to find ambulances and lorries waiting to carry them to Dimapur.

It was time for the weight of attack to be turned against the Japanese, who were still dug in among the sprawling houses in Kohima and the high ridges around the north and east of the town. They made renewed and desperate efforts to capture the town, but their infantrymen were mowed down by gunfire and blasted by the fighter-bombers. Troops of the 2nd British Division then assaulted the ridges in which the Japanese had dug bunkers, trenches and foxholes. There were heavy losses on both sides, and eventually tanks were brought up to blast the Japanese out of their positions. A brigade of the 7th Indian Division under Major-General Frank Messervy flew in from the Arakan and by 4 May was taking part in these operations, while the rest of its division was in transit. A brigade from XXXIII Corps, the 23rd Chindits under Brigadier L.E.C.M. Perowne, had arrived at Jorhat in the north along the railway and was under orders to move south-east round the enemy and cut off communications. These reinforcements would give the Allies a two-to-one numerical superiority over the Japanese 31st Division.

The fighting within and around Kohima was bloody and prolonged. The Japanese fought with their usual stubborn fanaticism, refusing to give way and even attacking against impossible odds. There were very heavy casualties on both sides, although the Allies attempted to lessen these by attacking behind smokescreens. Most of the area had been cleared by mid-May and Stopford ordered some more ambitious manoeuvres. The 7th Indian Division was sent eastwards through jungle terrain towards Jessami, while the 23rd Chindit Brigade circled further round to the east, in order to cut off the Japanese supply routes from Burma. The 2nd British Division was ordered to fight its way down the road to Imphal and destroy the Japanese defences in that direction, thus linking up with the troops of IV Corps.

Meanwhile Imphal had become a centre of intense fighting. Although this was on a larger scale than that at Kohima, there was less danger. Slim had taken the precaution of evacuating about 22,500 non-combatants, partly to avoid feeding them during an anticipated period of encirclement. He also continued to fly in reinforcements for the 17th, 20th and 23rd Indian Divisions of IV Corps already in the area. The headquarters and two brigades of the 5th Indian Division completed their fly-in by 22 March and these were soon followed by a battalion of Sikhs. A brigade of the 7th Indian Division from the Arakan was delayed by bad weather and did not arrive until 12 May. Supplies were brought in by the transport aircraft of the Troop Carrier Command, but the troops on the ground had become so numerous that they had to be put on half rations for a while.

The Japanese 15th and 31st Divisions headed the attacks, full of confidence and expecting to annihilate their enemy and capture supplies. However, when they descended from the jungle-clad hills and entered the plain, they were met with huge barrages from artillery, machine-guns, rifles, grenades and strafing from the air. When they were repulsed, the Allied tanks rolled up the hillsides ahead of the infantry and blasted their bunkers, foxholes and artillery positions, leaving hundreds of dead. The Japanese made no progress from investing

Imphal and suffered the major problem of bringing up supplies and reinforcements via lines which were under constant attack by the RAF and the USAAF. One of the Hurricane squadrons even managed to deliver attacks on their relief columns at night, guided by the headlights of their transports or solely by moonlight.

The Japanese showed signs of weakening during May, making smaller but still costly attacks. Towards the end of that month an Order of the Day signed by Lieutenant-General T. Tanaka, who had taken over command of the 33rd Division, was found on bodies of their soldiers. He exhorted them to make greater efforts in the knowledge that 'death was lighter than a feather' and that commanders 'may have to use their swords as a weapon of punishment' on those who shirked their duty. This was to no avail, for they were being counter-attacked, with the 20th Indian Division beginning to advance towards Ukhrul, a centre for the Japanese about 40 miles north-east of Imphal. Other infantrymen of IV Corps began to fight their way up the road to Kohima and on 22 June met tanks of the 2nd British Division moving south towards them. Thereafter Imphal could be supplied by road from Assam as well as by air.

For many months Tokyo radio had provided entertainment for the British and Indian troops in the form of propaganda relayed by a woman they dubbed 'Tokyo Rose'. She regularly announced in English the remarkable successes achieved by Japanese forces, evidently from advance timetables provided for her, and she did so during these operations. However, these did not correspond with reality and often gave notice of Japanese intentions which never came to fruition. The troops were able to laugh at her announcements, which convinced them of the stupidity of their enemy. The orders of both XXXIII Corps and IV Corps were to destroy the 15th Japanese Army west of the Chindwin river and they continued with this task in the certainty of victory.

The monsoon broke as usual, and the Allied troops were hampered by sticky mud as much as 18 inches deep. The cohesion of the enemy was disintegrating, although their scattered units continued to fight to the death. Ukhrul was surrounded by 1 July, a town that the enemy hoped would be the centre for reinforcements being sent into Burma at the rate of about 6,000 a month. All resistance there was crushed by mid-July and the remnants of the Japanese 15th and 31st Divisions began a rapid retreat to the Chindwin, following jungle paths and leaving much equipment behind. Piles of their dead were left in the villages in which the Allies arrived, lying in grisly heaps after dying of wounds, disease or starvation. Some of them had been shot through the head by their surviving comrades to prevent their capture. Large pits had to be dug as communal graves for such groups of bodies.

Further south, the 23rd Indian Division was pursuing and attacking two Japanese brigades, one from the 15th Division and the other from the 33rd. It entered Tamu at the end of July to find the rotting corpses of over 500 Japanese, as well as another 100 dying from wounds and starvation. The 23rd

On 6 August 1944 troops of the 2nd British Division, Fourteenth Army, captured the Burmese village of Tamu on the border with India. This photograph shows the winding road leading up to Tamu, which was followed by the retreating Japanese 15th Army.

Author's collection

Indian Division was then withdrawn for recuperation and was replaced by the 11th East African Division under the command of Major-General C.C. Fowkes, which had arrived from the Fourteenth Army Reserve at Chittagong. The East Africans continued the rout of the Japanese in this area and on 11 September entered Sittaung on the Chindwin river.

The other brigades of the Japanese 33rd Division were retreating southwards from Imphal, down the road towards Tiddim, but frequently turning to fight their pursuers. These were the troops of the 5th Indian Division, relieving the men of the 17th Indian Division which had been withdrawn for a rest. The RAF was very active in this sector, strafing those Japanese who still showed plenty of fight. These Japanese were eventually defeated by outflanking tactics and lost heavily.

The battles in the Central Front were costly to the Allies, despite their victories. The official figures gave a total of 17,587 battle casualties between November 1943 and July 1944, but these included a very large proportion of the wounded who were brought to safety and recovery. The RAF lost many aircrew, particularly from the close support provided for the troops and low-level attacks against communications, which were met with point-blank fire from the ground. From January to July 1944 as many as 97 Hurricanes were lost, as well as 38 Beaufighters, 34 Spitfires and 15 Vengeances. The Dakota squadrons lost 32 aircraft.

However, the losses suffered by the Japanese 15th Army on the Central Front were disastrous. According to their own figures, 84,280 men served in the army in this period, excluding reinforcements and those in the Indian National Army. Their losses were 53,505, of whom 30,502 had died and the remainder were wounded. Probably most of the latter did not recover in the prevailing conditions. They had also lost almost all their tanks and vehicles, while the Allies had captured 250 of their guns, in addition to those lost in rivers and jungles. They had been out-generalled and out-fought, and would never fully recover. It was time for the Allies to begin the reconquest of Burma by the land routes available to them.

(*Left*) Major-General H.R. Briggs, Commander of the 5th Indian Division from 16 November 1943 to 11 July 1944.
Author's collection

(*Below*) Major-General C.E.N. Lomax, Commander of the 26th Indian Division from 16 November 1943 to 20 March 1945, talking to Lieutenant-General A.F.P. Christison, Commander of XV Corps from 16 November 1943 to 30 September 1945.
Author's collection

(*Right*) A howitzer near a headquarters unit of the Fourteenth Army on the Arakan front carrying out harassing fire at Japanese positions.
Author's collection

(*Below*) Smoke from shell bursts on Japanese positions in the distant hills, 7 miles south of Maungdaw on the Arakan front, during bombardment in February 1944 by 3-inch mortars and 3.7-inch howitzers of the Fourteenth Army.
Author's collection

Men of the Burma Intelligence Corps studying a map of Japanese positions in the Ngakydauk Pass area of the Arakan Front in February 1944. The officer in the photograph knew the country well, having campaigned in it during the previous year. He had been taken prisoner by the Japanese but managed to escape. *Author's collection*

A tank of the Fourteenth Army driving forward with its guns blazing at Japanese camouflaged positions in the Ngakydauk Pass area of the Arakan Front in February 1944.

Author's collection

Supplies for the Fourteenth Army on the Arakan Front being carried on mules through a stream on the slopes of the Mayu Ridge, south of the Maungdaw–Buthidaung road, in February 1944.
Author's collection

(*Above*) Gurkhas from the 7th Indian Division of the Fourteenth Army, armed with kukris and fixed bayonets on their rifles, being briefed before setting out to hunt for Japanese patrols near the Ngakydauk Pass in the Arakan area of Northern Burma. The photograph is dated 29 February 1944.

Author's collection

(*Opposite top*) The Supermarine Spitfire VC, such as serial EE627 seen here, was a 'tropicalised' version that served in the Burma theatre. It was normally armed with four machine-guns and two cannon. The wings were capable of taking two 250lb bombs, or a 500lb bomb could be carried under the fuselage. Alternatively, long-range belly fuel tanks could be carried. A Vokes air filter was fitted under the engine cowling. This variant had a maximum speed of 374mph, a service ceiling of 37,000ft and a combat range of 1,135 miles.

Author's collection

(*Opposite bottom*) When the 7th Indian Division of the Fourteenth Army, commanded by Major-General Frank Messervy, was cut off in the so-called 'Admin Box' in north-west Burma for eleven days from 5 February 1944, supplies were dropped by the Troop Carrier Command led by Brigadier-General William D. Old of the USAAF. This photograph shows parachutes and containers lying on the ground, with a Dakota flying overhead.

Author's collection

Bombardier Gurune of the Fourteenth Army, photographed on the Arakan Front in January 1944.

Author's collection

A Japanese soldier, probably wounded, surrendering in February 1944 to a patrol of the 7th Indian Division, Fourteenth Army, in the Ngakydauk Pass area of the Arakan Front.

Author's collection

Gurkhas passing dead Japanese in the Ngakydauk Pass area of the Arakan Front in February 1944.

Author's collection

(*Above*) A Bren carrier crossing a ditch at full speed in the Ngakydauk Pass area, after the Japanese had been defeated in their attempt to encircle the 7th Indian Division in the 'Admin Box'.

Author's collection

(*Opposite top*) A West African driving a jeep with two other soldiers along a road hacked out of the jungle by his comrades in the Kaladan Valley, on the Arakan Front, in April 1944.

Author's collection

(*Opposite bottom*) The wounded and sick of the 7th Indian Division in the 'Admin Box' were lifted out by Dakotas and Commandos of the Troop Carrier Command, Air Command, South-East Asia. A USAAF crew member can be seen looking from the flight deck in this photograph.

Author's collection

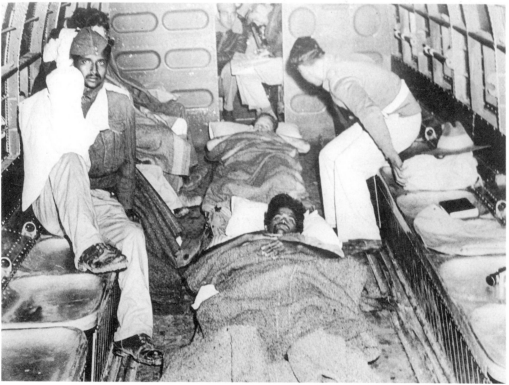

(*Above*) Colour Sergeant F. Wilson from Plymouth, smoking a home-made bamboo pipe, leading other men of his regiment in the Fourteenth Army on the Arakan Front in March 1944.
Author's collection

(*Opposite top*) A Vultee Vengeance of one of the RAF's squadrons within the 3rd Tactical Air Force, Eastern Air Command, being bombed up at a forward airfield in March 1944. The two-man crew had just landed after a successful dive-bombing attack against Japanese positions, in close support of the Fourteenth Army in Burma.
Author's collection

(*Opposite bottom*) Indian troops scrambling up a precipitous hillside in Arakan hill country during a fierce daylight attack against Japanese defenders in March 1944.
Author's collection

This photograph illustrates one method of bringing wounded men of the Fourteenth Army away from the combat area of the Burmese jungle in the Arakan area in early 1944. They were then taken by jeep, ambulance, air ambulance or river craft to hospitals in the rear.

Author's collection

The Stimson L-5 Sentinel was employed extensively in the Burma theatre of war. A two-seater with a very short take-off and landing facility, it was particularly suitable for sorties to jungle clearings. Most L-5s were supplied by the USAAF but the RAF had ordered a hundred of them, primarily for use in Burma. They conveyed VIPs, brought in supplies, with welcome additions such as newspapers for the troops, and took out casualties. The L-5 in this photograph served with the US Marine Corps in the Pacific.

Author's collection

Senior officers of Air Command, South-East Asia, photographed in May 1944. Left to right: Group Captain S.G. 'Bill' Wise (Commander, Photographic Reconnaissance Force); Air Marshal Sir Richard Pierse (Allied Air Commander-in-Chief); Lieutenant-General George E. Stratemeyer, USAAF (Air Commander, Eastern Air Command).

Wing Commander G.J. Craig collection

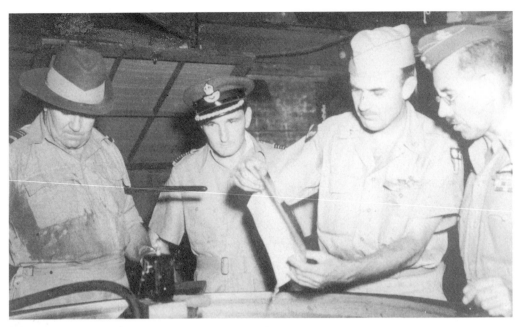

The USAAF Photographic Section at Bally in India, photographed in 1944. Left to right: Air Vice-Marshal T.M. Williams (Assistant Air Commander, Eastern Air Command); Group Captain S.G. Wise (Commander, Photographic Reconnaissance Force); Colonel Milton W. Kaye (Photographic Reconnaissance Force); Air Vice-Marshal R.V. Goddard (on visit from UK).

Wing Commander G.J. Craig collection

Spitfire PR XI serial PL773 of 681 Squadron at Dum-Dum in India, with two airmen sitting on the tailplane while the Merlin 61 engine was being run up. This mark of Spitfire arrived in the squadron in September 1943 and had a top speed of 417mph. It was painted in 'special blue'. Two vertical cameras were fitted in the rear fuselage, sometimes with the addition of an oblique camera for low-level work.

The late Group Captain S.G. Wise

Mingaladon airfield photographed by an Allied reconnaissance aircraft. This was the main airfield for Rangoon, situated a few miles north of the capital. Such photographs were taken to provide intelligence and also to act as target maps for bombing and strafing attacks.

Author's collection

(*Above*) Consolidated Liberators served with the RAF in the Burma theatre on special duties as well as in heavy bomber squadrons. This Liberator IIIA of 354 Squadron was photographed in 1944 at Cuttack in India, where the squadron was based from 17 August 1943 until moving to Minneriya in Ceylon on 12 October 1944. Fitted with long-range tanks, such aircraft were employed mainly on general reconnaissance and photographic work. They also attacked enemy shipping on occasions.

Wing Commander G.J. Craig collection

(*Opposite top*) An attack by RAF Beaufighters in March 1944 against craft on the Irrawaddy at Yethaya near Magwe, between Mandalay and Rangoon, set five of them ablaze. They were evidently loaded with petrol or oil for the Japanese forces.

Author's collection

(*Opposite bottom*) RAF Beaufighters attacking an oil barge with cannon and machine-gun fire at Steamer Point on the Irrawaddy near Pakokku, south-west of Mandalay.

Author's collection

(*Above*) The Republic P-47D Thunderbolt was employed by the RAF solely in the Burma theatre of war, where it began to replace the Hurricane fighter-bomber in May 1944. A single-seat fighter armed with eight .50-inch machine-guns and the capacity to carry three 500lb bombs, it was fitted with long-range tanks to attack Japanese troop positions and supply lines. Eventually sixteen RAF squadrons were equipped with Thunderbolts.

Author's collection

(*Opposite top*) A squadron of Republic P-47D Thunderbolts setting out on a sortie.

Author's collection

(*Opposite bottom*) Spitfire PR XIs of 681 Squadron being serviced at RAF Chandina in Assam, an airstrip close to the Burmese border. This was built without runways, hard-standings or permanent buildings, and was thus unusable in the monsoon period. The squadron was based there from 9 December 1943 to 30 January 1944, before returning to Dum-Dum near Calcutta.

Squadron Leader T.N. Rosser collection

An oil pumping station on the pipeline at Thegon, north-west of Moulmein, set on fire by RAF Beaufighters.

Author's collection

This suspension bridge carrying the oil pipeline between the Yenang-yaung oilfields to Syriam near Rangoon was set ablaze by RAF Beaufighters in April 1944.

Author's collection

The crew of a Vickers Wellington discussing the result of their raid on a Japanese strongpoint during the siege of Imphal in the state of Manipur, which took place during March and April 1944. The men were possibly serving with the RAF's 99 Squadron, part of Eastern Air Command's Strategic Air Force. This squadron was based at Jessore in East Bengal at the time, equipped with Wellington Xs and XIs.

Author's collection

Lord Louis Mountbatten made a tour of the forward battle area in June 1944. This photograph was taken at the camp site of the 5th Indian Division near Imphal, commanded by Major-General H.R. Briggs.
Author's collection

After the defeat of the Japanese at Kohima in late June 1944, British and Indian troops pushed further into Burma, despite the monsoon which was at its height in July. This photograph shows British troops combing elephant grass for Japanese snipers in the hilly country adjoining the Imphal plain, under cover of Bren gunfire.
Author's collection

Sergeant A. Beard of Manchester (left) and Private W. Pybis of Liverpool wading through a stream in full kit in September 1944 to relieve a forward outpost in Burma. Such men were often soaked to the skin in a fever-ridden jungle, as well as beset by leeches and vermin.

Author's collection

Men of the 10th Gurkha Rifles, having advanced along the road from Palel to Tamu in September 1944, clearing an enemy hill position known as 'Scraggy'. They were photographed moving forward past Japanese dead, equipment and caved-in bunkers.

Author's collection

The difficulties of fighting in the monsoon period are graphically illustrated by this photograph taken in September 1944 on the border between Palel in India and Tamu in Burma. Trucks and jeeps are moving forward along a muddy road while sappers and miners of a Bengal Field Company are clearing landslides.

Author's collection

British infantrymen in Burma working their way through a banana grove to root out Japanese troops in a 'basha' (bamboo hut) in November 1944.

Author's collection

CHAPTER FIVE

Crossing the Borders

While the battles in the Arakan, Kohima and Imphal were being fought, major engagements were also taking place in the Northern Combat Area Command (NCAC), so far distant that they almost constituted a separate war. On the Allied side the combatants were Major-General Orde Wingate's new 3rd Indian Division (Chindits), Lieutenant-General Joseph Stilwell's Chinese Army in India, his American Long-Range Penetration Regiment (Merrill's Marauders) and the Kachin Levies under his command in the area of Port Hertz. There was also the Chinese Army under separate command in their home territory of Yunnan. These various forces crossed the borders of Burma at different times and places, bringing the war to the vast northern area defended on the west by the 18th Division and on the east by the 56th Division, both part of the Japanese 33rd Army commanded by Lieutenant-General M. Honda.

The motives of the Americans in this theatre were different from those of the British. Their main objective was to ensure the safety of the Ledo Road being built from India over the mountains to connect with the northern stretch of the old Burma Road. They needed to eject the Japanese from this area, thus providing a land supply route to the Chinese fighting those invading their country. The British believed the best way to achieve this objective was the reconquest of the whole of Burma by land and air operations, and that the resources employed on the Ledo Road would be better engaged on building roads leading into Burma from Manipur and the Arakan. Then supplies could be brought in via Rangoon instead of Calcutta. However, the Anglo-American Combined Chiefs of Staff had decreed that the Ledo Road should be built, and the commanders in the field had to comply with this directive.

The first move to re-enter Burma in this theatre began in October 1943 when the Chinese 38th Division, commanded by Major-General Sun Li-jen, advanced southwards from Ledo. The Chinese made good progress in the first few weeks but then the Japanese opposition intensified and they stopped and dug in, following their usual practice. In overall command of the Chinese forces in India, Stilwell was not happy with this hold-up and on Christmas Day insisted on a further attack. This was successful and by the end of the year the Chinese 38th Division had reached a point over 100 miles from Ledo, with support on its right flank from a regiment of the Chinese 22nd Division commanded by Major-

General Liao Yao-hsiang. The remainder of the 22nd followed the 38th, together with a Chinese tank unit.

These two Chinese divisions then had welcome support from the 5307th Composite Regiment, consisting of three battalions of US infantry for long-range penetration operations behind Japanese lines. Commanded by Brigadier-General Frank D. Merrill and known as Merrill's Marauders, this group had spent three months training with Wingate's Chindits in central India and had been given the codename 'Galahad Force'. Its first task was to carry out medium-range operations after reaching Ledo on 9 February 1944. Its march southwards was followed by hooks and outflanking movements behind Japanese positions.

A very substantial operation in this theatre was planned by Wingate. His special force of Chindits had been expanded considerably. Although named the 3rd Indian Division, it had six brigades and was numerically the size of two divisions. It was composed mainly of British soldiers but there were also some Gurkhas and West Africans. They had been training intensively in central India and were ready to reinforce Stilwell's expeditions to protect the Ledo Road, but remained under the command of Slim's Fourteenth Army. One most unusual aspect of this large division was the support of a special air group, named No. 1 Air Commando and formed on 1 January 1944 under the command of Colonel Phillip Cochrane of the USAAF. It consisted of twelve B-25 Mitchell medium bombers, thirty P-51 Mustang long-range fighters, twenty-five DC-4 Dakota transports, about 110 L-1 or L-5 light aircraft for liaison operations, and 150 Waco CG-4A gliders. It soon became known as 'Cochrane's Circus' by the airmen who served in it.

Wingate's objective was to plant his Chindits well behind the Japanese positions, in natural clearings within the jungle around the little town of Indaw (known as Rail Indaw since it was on the railway line between Mandalay and Myitkyina). They would then be able to disrupt road, rail and river communications in north Burma, and thus assist the advance of Stilwell's Chinese-American forces as well as give the Chinese army in Yunnan an opportunity to enter Burma against limited opposition. Three of Wingate's six brigades would be in the first wave, one going in on foot and the other two carried by air. The other three brigades would be kept in reserve to reinforce or relieve the first wave. The whole operation was codenamed 'Thursday'.

The first of the Chindits to leave was the 16th British Brigade commanded by Brigadier Bernard E. Fergusson, which marched out of Ledo on 8 February 1944 on the long haul to a jungle clearing codenamed 'Aberdeen'. The 77th Indian Brigade under Brigadier J.M. Calvert and the 111th Indian Brigade under Brigadier W.D.A. Lentaigne were scheduled to fly from Lalaghat and Hailakandi airfields in north Assam to clearings codenamed 'Piccadilly', 'Broadway' and 'Chowringhee'. The first take-offs would begin from Lalaghat in the late afternoon of 5 March, before a night when there would be a full moon and probably a clear sky. Both Slim and Wingate were present to direct the operation.

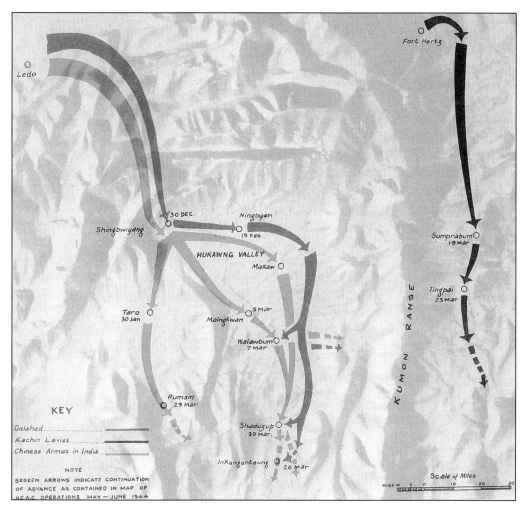

Operations on the Northern Front, November 1943–March 1944. This map is copied from the *Report to the Combined Chiefs of Staff by the Supreme Commander South-East Asia 1943–1945*, published by HMSO in 1951.

A few minutes before take-off an American air officer rushed up with a photograph taken shortly before, showing logs obstructing the clearing at 'Piccadilly'. It seemed at first that the Japanese had set a trap but photographs of the other clearings were clear and Slim soon decided to allow take-offs to proceed after Wingate had diverted the gliders scheduled for 'Piccadilly' to 'Broadway'. This decision was later proved to be correct, for the obstructions were merely the result of Burmese tree-fellers who had dragged teak logs to dry in the clearing.

Sixty-one Dakotas took off from Lalaghat during the evening and night, all headed for 'Broadway'. They carried men, equipment, ammunition and supplies. The first four gliders included the headquarters of the 77th Indian Brigade and a detachment of American airfield engineers. Each Dakota, flying as a tug, towed two gliders, although this overloading was questioned by some pilots. It was the beginning of the largest airborne operation in the Second World War, but this day did not go as well as planned. The first glider carried a wireless set, and the troops laid out a flare path. However, the ground was rutted and the next gliders crashed, the wreckage not being cleared before others arrived.

Of thirty-five gliders which landed at 'Broadway', only three were undamaged. Twenty-three men were killed and many others injured. But about 400 men landed safely, eventually clearing the wreckage and preparing an airstrip for later landings. With regard to the other gliders, four made crash-landings when their nylon towing ropes broke after take-off, eight were recalled and landed back safely, five others came down in Allied territory and the remaining nine in enemy territory.

The airstrip was ready by the following day, and Dakotas began to bring in further supplies, troops and mules. Light aircraft took the wounded back to safety. The entire brigade was gathered at 'Broadway' by the end of the next three days, without interference from the Japanese. An operation had also begun to occupy 'Chowringhee' which, unlike the other two airstrips, was east of the Irrawaddy.

Among the arrivals at 'Chowringhee' was a column named 'Morrisforce', consisting of the 4/9th Burma Rifles commanded by Lieutenant-Colonel J.R. Morris. This set out from the airstrip on 10 March on a long march eastwards, in order to blow up bridges leading to the Japanese troops at Myitkyina in the north. Two days later another column named 'Dahforce' marched out of 'Broadway' on a similar quest, eventually to link up with 'Morrisforce'. 'Dahforce' consisted of a mixture of British troops and Kachin levies. It was commanded by Lieutenant-Colonel D.C. Herring, who had had experience of the terrain and hoped to gather further support from local Burmese.

By 11 March the whole of the 111th Indian Brigade had arrived at 'Chowringhee' airstrip without any casualties, and Wingate ordered the men to march to 'Aberdeen', which the 16th British Brigade had reached after its long march from Ledo. A total of some 12,000 men had then been planted, in the words of Wingate, 'in the guts of the enemy'.

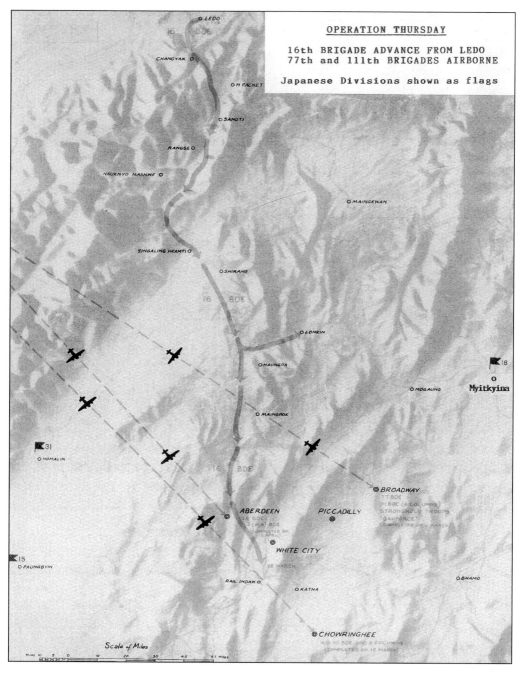

OPERATION THURSDAY

16th BRIGADE ADVANCE FROM LEDO
77th and 111th BRIGADES AIRBORNE

Japanese Divisions shown as flags

Operation 'Thursday'. This map is copied from the *Report to the Combined Chiefs of Staff by the Supreme Commander South-East Asia 1943–1945*, published by HMSO in 1951.

Even more troops arrived to support this operation. On 22 March Wingate's 3rd West African Brigade and the majority of his 14th British Brigade began to fly to 'Aberdeen'. The 14th was one of the two brigades of Wingate's 3rd Indian Division which had been diverted to assist the Fourteenth Army in the battles around Kohima and Imphal, but Slim agreed to relinquish most of its battalions. In addition, the Kachin Levies at Fort Hertz in the far north-east of Burma had been stiffened by the 4th Battalion of the Burma Regiment and began to move south, under the command of Colonel G.A. McGee. Their objective was to assist in the capture of Myitkyina from the Japanese, since this town was vital for the construction of the last stretch of the Ledo Road. Its nearby airfield was also important as a staging post for the transport aircraft on the 'Hump Run'. It would enable these to bypass the higher mountain peaks they were obliged to cross on the more direct route.

The Japanese reaction to all these movements was slow, since the majority of their 18th Division was heavily involved in the battle for Imphal. An air attack was made on 'Broadway' on 13 March, but by this time a flight of Spitfires was on detachment at the airstrip while an anti-aircraft battery was also in position. The Japanese lost half their aircraft.

Wingate's success ended in personal tragedy. After visiting his commanders in Burma early on 24 March, he flew to Imphal to discuss air operations with Air Marshal Sir John Baldwin. He then left Imphal in the late evening of the same day, flying in a B-25 Mitchell bomber of the USAAF to his new headquarters at Lalaghat, in company with two war reporters from London newspapers. The aircraft crashed in the mountains west of Imphal and all on board were killed. The reason for the accident is unknown, but the Mitchell came down on the reverse side of a ridge. Thus it seems to have been the result of either an engine failure or a strong down-current in an area prone to extreme weather conditions. Slim had the responsibility of appointing a successor and chose Brigadier W.D.A. Lentaigne, who was promoted to major-general, while his 111th Indian Brigade was taken over by Lieutenant-Colonel J.R. Morris, who was promoted to brigadier.

As previously arranged by Wingate, the 16th British Brigade marched out of 'Aberdeen' and on 26 March attempted to storm the Japanese positions at Indaw, supported by part of the 14th British Brigade. This was a maintenance and supply dump defended by Japanese garrison troops, who proved too well dug-in to prepared positions for the lightly armed Chindits without artillery. The attack was repulsed with heavy casualties. By then the Chindits of the 16th were exhausted after their long marches and other efforts. They were withdrawn by air shortly afterwards. However, the remaining Chindit brigades successfully cut many road and railway communications, fighting minor engagements with parties of Japanese and forming strongholds which they named 'White City' and 'Blackpool'. These were defended against artillery bombardments and fierce attacks. These operations tied up Japanese forces and to some extent hampered their supply route to the battle around Imphal.

When the rains began, some of the airstrips used to supply the Chindits became waterlogged and unsuitable for landings, but the RAF had an unusual remedy. Two Sunderland IIIs of 230 Squadron based at Koggala in Ceylon were detached from their anti-submarine duties and flown via Calcutta to the Brahmaputra river in northern Assam. Their interiors were prepared for carrying freight and 'casevac' operations. One arrived on 31 May and the other on 6 June. Between those dates and 4 July they made thirteen successful sorties to Indawgwi Lake, close to the Chindit positions, about 50 miles north-north-east of Rail Indaw. They brought in supplies and flew out the sick and wounded, often flying in monsoon conditions over mountains more than 11,000 feet in height, usually without fighter escort. The Chindits nicknamed the Sunderlands 'Gert and Daisy' after well-known music hall characters, but they certainly had reason to applaud the RAF since these two flying boats evacuated a total of 506 casualties.

Stilwell's Chinese forces had meanwhile made considerable progress, with his Marauders making short hooks round enemy positions to attack them from the rear. The old warrior was presented with two extra Chinese divisions, the 14th and the 50th, which were flown into Assam from China during mid-April. Thus he had five divisions plus his long-range Marauders, although the new arrivals were inexperienced troops. The next objective of the Marauders was a long march eastwards to Myitkyina, supplied from the air.

The transport aircraft were so heavily involved with air lifts to the Allied troops defending Kohima and Imphal that the resources available for this additional task were limited. Nevertheless the three battalions of Marauders set off on 28 April, together with six Chinese battalions, on a march of almost 100 miles over wild country which included a trackless mountain range some 6,000 feet in height, beset at times by heavy rain which turned the ground into sticky mud. They reached the airfield at Myitkyina on 17 May and took the small Japanese garrison by surprise. After a sharp engagement the latter withdrew into the nearby town, where they joined their main force.

On the same day Slim placed all his troops in this theatre under Stilwell's command, since the capture of Myitkyina was the prime objective of this part of the Allied campaign. The Marauders and the Chinese were almost completely exhausted by their long march, and indeed Merrill himself collapsed soon afterwards and was no longer able to lead them, but Chinese reinforcements were rapidly flown into the captured airfield.

The Japanese in Myitkyina rapidly drew in reinforcements from the surrounding area until they numbered some 3,500 men from their 18th and 56th Divisions. The detachment advancing from Fort Hertz was unable to prevent this reinforcement, nor was the combined 'Morrisforce/Dahforce' moving up from the south. Commanded by Major-General G. Mizukami of the 56th, the Japanese in Myitkyina fought with great skill and courage against the newly arrived Chinese regiments, which launched their first attack on 19 May without making any progress.

Merrill's Marauders captured Myitkyina airfield on 17 May 1944, after an extremely exhausting twenty-day march of 100 miles through thick jungle and over steep hills. Other troops and supplies were immediately flown in. In this photograph a Dakota is taking off during a counter-attack by Mitsubishi 'Zeros'. Another Dakota is on fire in the background and a dead Japanese soldier is lying in the foreground.

Author's collection

Meanwhile Generalissimo Chiang Kai-shek had at last decided to launch an assault from Yunnan. About 40,000 Chinese troops began to cross the Salween river on the night of 10/11 May, on a very broad front. These were soon followed by about 32,000 additional troops, thus forming an army totalling twelve divisions under the command of General Wei Li Huang. They needed to work their way through mountain passes defended by the 56th Division, consisting of 12,000 troops under Lieutenant-General S. Matsuyama. The Japanese positions had been well prepared and the troops fought with their usual skill and dedication, holding off the attackers throughout May and early June before falling back gradually. The Chinese were hampered by their long lines of communication and poor supply organisation, while their troops even lacked proper clothing. Although they made some progress with their immense numerical superiority, the Japanese were still holding out in this region by the end of August, at the cost of some 3,000 battle casualties.

Stilwell fumed and fretted while his Chinese and Americans failed to break through at Myitkyina, blaming his commanders for lack of aggression. His special forces were gradually withdrawn after months of effort, as were 'Morrisforce' and the Chindits in the western areas. The 36th Indian Division commanded by Major-General F.W. Festing, which had been refitting in Assam, was flown in during July to replace the Chindits and placed under Stilwell's command as a temporary measure.

Myitkyina was bombed and strafed by No. 1 Air Commando but the diminishing force of Japanese still held out, following their usual creed of fighting to the death. The siege continued until 3 August, two days after Mizukami had ordered the remainder of his garrison, amounting to about 800 men, to break out. All except a small number too ill to move attempted to escape on rafts down the Irrawaddy but most were killed. Only about 200 managed to get clear. Meanwhile Mizukami remained in the town and committed suicide.

The main objective of the campaign had been achieved at last, and the building of the Ledo Road could continue. The total cost of its construction was recorded as 137 million dollars, a huge sum in those days. A vast area of land held by the Japanese had fallen to the Allies, partly because so many of their troops were engaged elsewhere on their fruitless 'March on Delhi'. The battle casualties suffered by the Chindits up to July 1944 were recorded as 3,628 killed, wounded or missing. Figures given by the Americans recorded 13,618 Chinese and 1,327 American battle casualties between 1 January and 19 August 1944. These numbers included the wounded who were flown out for further treatment. It was estimated that 22,000 Japanese were killed in this part of the campaign in north Burma.

Meanwhile the Strategic Air Force of SEAC, commanded by Brigadier-General H.C. Davidson of the USAAF, had been extremely active during the battles on the Central and Northern Fronts, employing its USAAF and RAF squadrons of long-range B-24 Liberators and medium-range B-25 Mitchells and Wellingtons.

This force was small numerically, averaging only about eighty heavy and fifty medium bombers during the period, but it carried out some steady work, particularly in the disruption of Japanese communications in more distant areas. It thus complemented the work of the 3rd Tactical Air Force which gave close support to the troops on the ground.

Some of the most effective work consisted of mine-laying, dropping magnetic mines in shallow waters during moonlit nights. These mines rested on the sea bottom and exploded when the metal hull of a vessel passed over them. The main dropping zones were in the narrows of the Strait of Malacca between Malaya and Sumatra, off the ports along the west coast of the Kra Isthmus and in the Gulf of Martaban south of Rangoon. These brought enemy sea traffic almost to a halt, since the few merchant vessels remaining to the Japanese could not be risked. Small and light coastal craft were employed, but most supplies to Burma had to be brought overland.

Most of the other strategic air operations took place in daylight, since the Japanese fighters had been almost swept from the skies by this time. It was calculated that the number of sorties flown by the Allies in this period was thirty times higher than those of the Japanese. Attacks were made on port installations, factories and the oil wells of Yenangyaung. Perhaps the most important targets were the railways, which were vulnerable where they passed across bridges over rivers and gorges. The most notorious of these railways was the line built by slave labour from Bangkok and Moulmein, in which thousands of British, Australian, American and Dutch prisoners-of-war died from sadistic treatment, malnutrition and sickness. One recorded example of this cruelty concerned 7,000 prisoners brought from Singapore to Siam in April 1943. About 3,100 of these were dead within a year.

The railway bridges in Siam and Burma were bombed continually by the Strategic Air Force. The major bridge over the Sittang and the Ava bridge over the Irrawaddy, both of which had been blown by the Allies during their retreat, were always kept out of action. However, bridges were small targets to hit from high level and the Japanese were always adept at making repairs or improvising temporary crossings across rivers. The tonnage carried on the railways increased, although it would have been much higher without this continual hindrance.

The Royal Navy's Eastern Fleet based in Ceylon assumed a far more aggressive role during this period. The collection of ancient warships which faced the Japanese Navy in 1942 had been withdrawn to the east coast of Africa and replaced with a formidable array of battleships, battle cruisers, fleet carriers, aircraft carriers, destroyers, depot ships and submarines, all under the command of Admiral Sir James Somerville. Most of these had become available after the surrender of the Italian Navy in September 1943. The main menace faced by the fleet in the Indian Ocean during early 1944 was the German U-boats and Japanese submarines which preyed on merchant vessels and troop transports, giving considerable cause for concern. Some of these enemy submarines were

RAF Liberators of the Strategic Air Force, Eastern Air Command, making low-level attacks on one of two road bridges between Pegu and Martaban, which had been built to supply Japanese forces on the Mandalay and Arakan Fronts. The photograph shows smoke from bomb explosions and debris floating in the river after wooden trestles had collapsed. The other road bridge had already been cut.

Author's collection

sunk while those of the Eastern Fleet were achieving results. A success came on 11 January 1944 when the submarine HMS *Tally Ho!* torpedoed and sank the Japanese light cruiser *Kuma* off Penang. This was followed up on 26 January when the submarine HMS *Templar* torpedoed and badly damaged the Japanese cruiser *Kitagami*, also off Penang.

In early April the US Chief of Naval Operations, Admiral E.J. King, requested an attack on some suitable target in the Andaman Islands in order to occupy the attention of the Japanese fleet in Singapore while General Douglas MacArthur carried out amphibious reconquests in the Pacific. However, Admiral Somerville had already organised a more ambitious assault against the naval base on Sabang Island on the north-west tip of Sumatra. This began on 16 April when two carriers, three battleships, six cruisers and twelve destroyers left Ceylon. The carriers were HMS *Illustrious* and USS *Saratoga*, under the command of Vice-Admiral Sir Arthur Power in the cruiser HMS *Renown*, while the supporting battleship force was commanded by Admiral Somerville. Three days later the fleet was in position about 100 miles south-west of Sabang, and forty-six bombers with twenty-seven fighters were flown off. These achieved complete surprise and sank one merchant ship, damaged another, set fire to three oil tanks, and probably destroyed twenty-one enemy aircraft on the ground. One fighter from *Saratoga* came down in the sea but the pilot was rescued by an escorting submarine. All the warships returned safely.

An operation at very long range then took place when the Eastern Fleet sailed from Ceylon on 6 May, this time against the oil refinery and engineering works at Sourabaya on the north-eastern tip of Java. The fleet reached the north-west tip of Australia on 15 May and then headed due north. On 19 May, when about 100 miles south-west of Sourabaya, nineteen bombers with twenty fighters were flown off to attack the harbour, while twenty-six bombers and twenty fighters set off for the oil refinery. They caused much destruction, although one fighter was shot down. All the warships returned safely, having steamed about 7,000 miles in twenty-two days without defects in their engine rooms.

In early June Admiral King repeated his request for an attack against the Andamans. This took place when the fleet carrier HMS *Illustrious* left Ceylon on 17 June in company with the French battleship *Richelieu* and the heavy cruiser HMS *Renown*, plus attendant vessels. When about 90 miles from Port Blair in the Andaman Islands four days later, twenty-four Vought Corsairs and fifteen Fairey Barracudas were flown off to bomb the harbour and airfield. These took the defences by surprise but two aircraft were lost, although the pilot of one was picked up by a submarine escort.

Two more fleet carriers joined the Eastern Fleet in July, HMS *Victorious* and HMS *Indomitable*, but since the Japanese had not responded to carrier-borne attacks, Admiral Somerville thought it advisable to provoke them with a gun bombardment of shore positions. He again chose Sabang and personally led the operation in the battleship HMS *Queen Elizabeth*. The fleet left Ceylon on 22 July and arrived off the target three days later. Thirty-four Corsairs were flown off the carriers HMS *Illustrious* and HMS *Victorious*, some to attack the airfields and a radar station while others provided cover for the warships as they closed in. Four battleships and a battle cruiser then pounded the harbour installations with 15-inch shells while five other cruisers engaged the shore batteries. Then another cruiser and three destroyers entered the harbour itself, firing torpedoes at vessels and engaging the port with gunfire at short range. All the warships returned safely, although two of the destroyers and their accompanying cruiser received slight damage. The operation was a fitting finale for Admiral Somerville, who ended his tour of duty on 22 August and was replaced by Admiral Sir Bruce Fraser.

Although the Eastern Fleet had become dominant in the Indian Ocean and the Bay of Bengal, its employment in any amphibious invasion of Rangoon was not immediately possible, since all the landing craft had been sent to the European theatre for the Anglo-American invasion of Normandy in June 1944. The commanders of SEAC had no option but to follow up their recent advantages with a continuation of land operations. By October 1944 it was decided the first phase should be a drive southwards by the Northern Combat Area Command coupled with an advance eastwards by the Fourteenth Army across the Chindwin, codenamed operation 'Capital'. There would also be an advance down the Arakan, codenamed operation 'Romulus'. After these were accomplished, probably in March 1945, Akyab would be captured and the next phase would be an amphibious operation from there, codenamed operation 'Dracula', resulting in the reoccupation of Rangoon.

Some arrangements in the Allied command structure were made to facilitate their plans. One problem was the lack of troop reinforcements for the British divisions, owing to the great land battles taking place on the European mainland. Their battalions needed to be whittled down, while more Indian battalions had to be created. Other recommendations were made by General Sir George Gifford of the Eleventh Army Group before his tour of duty came to an end on 12 November 1944. This Group was then renamed Allied Land Forces, South-East Asia (ALFSEA) with Lieutenant-General Sir Oliver Leese as the Commander-in-Chief. Gifford recommended that Lieutenant-General Slim should be relieved of some responsibilities so that he and his Fourteenth Army could concentrate on the push into the Central Front. Thus XV Corps operating in the Arakan under Lieutenant-General Christison was transferred from Slim to the direct control of Sir Oliver Leese. At the same time a Lines of Communication Command was formed to relieve Slim of the huge amount of administrative work required for operation 'Capital'.

An unexpected change came on 18 October when Lieutenant-General Joseph W. Stilwell was recalled to the USA. This followed a loss of confidence in his ability expressed by the Generalissimo, who irrationally blamed him for the failure to mount an amphibious operation against Rangoon. His place as commander of the Chinese forces in the India–Burma area was taken over by his former deputy, Lieutenant-General D.I. Sultan, while his position as Deputy Supreme Allied Commander was taken over by Lieutenant-General R.A. Wheeler of the US Army. Lieutenant-General Sir Adrian Carton de Wiart, who had considerable knowledge of Chinese affairs, took over the position of Representative with the Generalissimo.

There were also some changes in the Japanese command structure, although these were not known to the Allies for several months. They were made on 30 August after the failure of their 'March on Delhi'. Lieutenant-General T. Kawabe was sent home in disgrace and his place as Commander-in-Chief of the Burma Area Army was taken over by Lieutenant-General H. Kimura, 68 years of age and a former artillery officer who had been Vice-Minister of War in Tokyo from April 1941 to March 1943. Lieutenant-General R. Mutaguchi of the 15th Army was replaced by Lieutenant-General S. Katamura. Evidently it was hoped that these changes would result in an improvement of fortunes in any forthcoming battles on the Central Front.

The Fourteenth Army under Slim was thus confined to IV Corps and XXXIII Corps, so that all his efforts could be concentrated on the advance over the Chindwin river. He set up his headquarters in Imphal, together with Air Vice-Marshal S.F. Vincent in command of 221 Group, part of the RAF's 3rd Tactical Air Force. In this period Vincent's group consisted of fourteen squadrons equipped with Hurricanes, Spitfires and Thunderbolts and one with Mosquitos. He could also call on 224 Group if need be, commanded by Air Vice-Marshal the Earl of Bandon. This group consisted of thirteen squadrons equipped with Beaufighters, Hurricanes, Thunderbolts and Spitfires and a single squadron of P-38 Lightnings.

Slim needed to select the ground forces for this advance. From IV Corps, then commanded by Lieutenant-General G.A.P. Scoones, he allocated the 7th and 19th Indian Divisions, together with the 255th Tank Brigade. From XXXIII Corps, commanded by Lieutenant-General M.G.N. Stopford, he allocated the 2nd British Division, the 20th Indian Division, the 268th Brigade and the 254th Tank Brigade. Three bridgeheads over the Chindwin were established for their advance, at Sittaung in the north, at Mawlaik further south, and at Kalewa south of Mawlaik.

It was estimated that the Japanese forces opposing the Fourteenth Army would consist of four divisions, three of which had been badly mauled during the battle of Imphal but subsequently brought up to strength with reinforcements of less experienced troops. Together with other units such as lines of communication personnel, the Japanese would probably number about 50,000 men, but they lacked armour and air cover. Slim hoped that, once his forces had crossed the Chindwin and the range of hills beyond, these Japanese would stand and fight in the open area north-west of Mandalay, known as the Shwebo Plain. This open area suited the tactics favoured by British and Indian forces, especially

Lieutenant-General H. Kimura, who was appointed by the Japanese High Command as Commander-in-Chief of the Burma Area Army on 30 August 1944.

Author's collection

when strongly backed by tanks, artillery and air cover. The backs of the Japanese forces would be against a long loop of the wide Irrawaddy river, making any retreat difficult, and they would be wiped out.

In anticipation of the continuing defeat of the remaining Japanese forces, many groups of special agents were dropped behind their lines. This form of activity was not new, for several agents had been dropped by parachute or landed by submarine in South-East Asia since 1942. On 1 June 1943 the RAF had formed 1576 Flight for this purpose, equipped with Hudsons. This flight became 357 Squadron on 1 February 1944, based at Digri west of Calcutta. It then received Liberators and Catalinas to add to its Hudsons, with its flight of Catalinas operating from Redhills Lake near Madras. Dakotas also arrived the following December. By this time the aircraft were flying from various airfields on clandestine missions over Burma, Malaya, Siam and French Indo-China, dropping agents and supplies.

These special agents needed extraordinary courage to carry out this type of work, for if captured they faced hideous torture from the Japanese before execution. They were the Far East extension of the Special Operations Executive in London, and SEAC gave them the codename 'Force 136'. One of their tasks was to provide intelligence on matters such as Japanese dispositions and lines of communication, but they were also active in raising resistance groups to harry the Japanese. The north of Burma had been one of their main areas in 1943, where they had been partially responsible for the formation of the Kachin Levies who marched from Fort Hertz to Myitkyina.

In late 1944 the number of these agents was increased as men with experience of similar work in France, before that country had been liberated by the Allies, were brought in. These men were known as Jedburghs but had no connection with that town in the Scottish borders. Most were British, American or French, recruited from various branches of the armed services. All had been trained at Milton Hall in Peterborough in Northamptonshire. Several were the survivors of those dropped earlier in France or the Low Countries. They had become available for the Far East following a visit to India by their commanding officer, Lieutenant-Colonel G.R. Musgrave.

The special agents were dropped into Burma in groups of three, each group being given a codename and consisting of an officer in charge, another who could speak the local Burmese dialect, and a wireless operator with a portable set capable of transmitting or receiving messages in Morse and fitted with its own hand generator. Most of the newly arrived Jedburghs were British and were dropped from January 1945 onwards, following some training in the extremely difficult and unpleasant conditions of tropical jungles.

The advances over the Chindwin were also preceded by extensive activity from the RAF's Photographic Reconnaissance Force, commanded by Group Captain S.G. Wise. Some of these aircraft had taken a series of line-overlaps of areas which were inadequately mapped, so that mosaics could be created for intelligence purposes. The RAF's 3rd Tactical Air Force had also been very active, attacking Japanese communications and depots, before beginning close support of the Fourteenth Army in its advances.

Operation 'Capital' began on 3 December 1944 when a brigade of XXXIII Corps' 20th Indian Division commanded by Major-General D.D. Cracey crossed the Chindwin via the Mawlaik bridgehead about 30 miles north of Kalewa. Within the next fortnight almost all the attacking forces had crossed via the three bridgeheads. These were the remainder of the 20th Indian Division, XXXIII Corps' 2nd British Division commanded by Major-General C.G.G. Nicholson, and IV Corps' 19th Indian Division commanded by Major-General T.G. Rees. The crossing at Kalewa was facilitated by a long Bailey Bridge constructed by 10 December.

On 14 December Slim and two corps commanders, Stopford and Scoones, were knighted by the Viceroy of India, with special permission from King George VI. By this time Lieutenant-General Frank W. Messervy had succeeded Scoones as the commander of IV Corps.

Slim had expected strong opposition from the Japanese 15th Army when his divisions crossed the Chindwin but in the event this proved surprisingly light.

British and Indian troops of IV Corps, Fourteenth Army, marching east to the jungle-covered hills after crossing the Chindwin river at Sittaung in mid-December 1944.

Author's collection

Contrary to their usual tactics, the Japanese kept retreating while merely leaving rearguards to delay the attackers. There were some vicious clashes with these as well as the need to deal with a few suicide squads left behind and armed with mines, but in general the Japanese forces avoided contact while their retreat was steady and orderly.

Thus the troops advancing on the Central Front made rapid progress. The 19th Indian Division, which had passed through the Sittaung bridgehead on 4 December and then marched east, had covered about 85 miles twelve days later. Its advanced patrols then made contact near Rail Indaw with the 36th British Division from the Northern Combat Area Command. The 36th, which had been redesignated from 'Indian' to 'British' on 1 September, was under the command of Major-General F.W. Festing and had fought its way down the railway corridor from Myitkyina. This was the first link-up between the Allied forces on the Northern and Central Fronts.

Both the 20th Indian Division and the 2nd British Division also raced ahead, with the latter seizing Ye-U and its airfield on 2 January 1945. The 19th Indian Division continued its advance and captured the town and airfield of Shwebo on 7 January. By this time the whole of the Shwebo Plain was in the hands of the attackers but there had been no major battles with the Japanese. There had been few Allied battle casualties but many men had been incapacitated by sickness when moving through fever-ridden jungles.

It was apparent to Slim in the early stages of these advances that the Japanese had changed their tactics. This was confirmed by RAF air reconnaissance of their positions and then from documents found on prisoners or dead bodies. Under the new command of Lieutenant-General Kimura, they had pulled back all the divisions of their 15th Army and one of their 33rd Army to set up strong defensive positions along the eastern banks of the Irrawaddy protecting Mandalay. Kimura hoped that the attackers would squander their strength on fruitless attempts to cross this wide river under heavy fire and that he could mount a counter-attack when they were forced to retreat during the next monsoon.

Of course, Slim had no intention of falling into this trap. He modified a contingency plan made beforehand and issued new instructions to both his corps commanders. The divisions of XXXIII Corps, plus the 19th Division of IV Corps, were to cross the Irrawaddy well to the north of Mandalay, as a diversionary measure. The main attack would come from IV Corps much further south at Pakokku, about 20 miles beyond the point where the Chindwin flowed into the Irrawaddy. Having crossed this river, the Corps would strike south-east and capture Meiktila, the main base from which supplies reached Mandalay, and thus cut off the whole of the Japanese forces in that area. The forces would then turn north to the rear of the Japanese around Mandalay, eventually crushing them.

The next operation would be an amphibious assault to recapture Rangoon. This plan involved a long haul southwards from Tamu in Burma by IV Corps. It passed along a rough road, 328 miles long, to the west of the Chindwin, and depended partly on supplies from the air. But a sudden problem arose when news arrived from China of a Japanese push which threatened the loss of Kunming. On 10 December, in response to an urgent request from the Generalissimo, Mountbatten had to release two of the Chinese divisions from the Northern Front, as well as three of the Combat Carrier squadrons, including two allotted for Slim's revised 'Capital' operation.

The loss of these Dakotas was a blow to Slim's plans but he devised a partial remedy by turning to a method of river transport along the Chindwin and eventually along the Irrawaddy. He worked on this scheme with his Chief Engineer, Brigadier W.F. Hasted. A boat-building yard was immediately formed on a bank of the Chindwin at Kalewa, utilising timber from local trees and prefabricated parts with outboard motors from the Inland Water Transport Service in Calcutta. Progress was rapid, with some craft salvaged from the river bottom. Three small

The boat-building factory at Kalewa on the Chindwin river, photographed by the RAF. Work began on its establishment at the end of December 1944 by the Inland Water Transport Service.
Squadron Leader J.D. Braithwaite collection

rafts lashed together could carry a Sherman tank. It later transpired that supplies carried from Kalewa down the Chindwin by these improvised craft rose steadily from a daily average of 76 tons in February 1945 to 662 tons by the following May. Two larger vessels were fitted with guns and even flew the White Ensign, but without permission from the Admiralty.

Two divisions and three brigades of IV Corps were ordered to begin this long march on 19 December 1944. They were the 7th Indian Division commanded by Lieutenant-General C.C. Evans, the 17th Indian Division commanded by Lieutenant-General D.T. Cowan, the 255th Indian Tank Brigade equipped with Sherman tanks and commanded by Brigadier C.E. Pert, the 28th East African Brigade commanded by Brigadier W.A. Dimoline, and the Lushai Brigade commanded by Brigadier P.C. Marindin. All these forces had been in reserve save the Lushai Brigade, which had been formed from spare Indian battalions and some levies. This had been harrying the Japanese for several months during their advance into India and subsequent retreat.

It was essential that absolute secrecy was maintained if this plan were to succeed. Mountbatten later wrote 'Lieutenant-General Slim's plan, of which Lieutenant-General Leese and I entirely approved, was as brilliant in its conception as in its successful execution; for it laid the foundation for the complete destruction of the Japanese Army in Burma.'

(*Above*) American and Chinese troops (the latter wearing British helmets) of the Northern Combat Area Command, under General Joseph W. Stilwell of the US Army, advancing in early 1944.

Author's collection

(*Opposite top*) Chinese troops of the Northern Combat Area Command rushing headlong into an attack.

Author's collection

(*Opposite bottom*) Troops of Brigadier-General Frank D. Merrill's 5307th Composite Regiment, known as Merrill's Marauders, marching south from Ledo in February 1944 on their long-range penetration operation behind Japanese lines, in support of advancing Chinese divisions.

Author's collection

Advance units of Chinese troops, under the overall command of General Joseph W. Stilwell, carrying supplies while marching further into north Burma during March 1944.

Author's collection

(*Above*) Waco CG-4A gliders lined up on Lalaghat airfield in India on 5 March 1944, ready to be towed off by Dakotas of No. 1 Air Commando, Eastern Air Command, for the second Chindit expedition which began at moonrise in the late evening of the same day. Eighty of these American gliders were available for this expedition, which was codenamed operation 'Thursday'. Their tow-ropes were laid out neatly in line.

Author's collection

(*Right*) A Waco CG-4A glider being towed over the Chin Hills on operation 'Thursday'. The glider pilot would eventually slip the tow-rope when the designated clearing appeared in the jungle and then attempt to skid to a landing.

Author's collection

Chindits, dressed in their green uniforms and carrying a wounded comrade on a stretcher, returning from their part in operation 'Thursday'.

Author's collection

Bombing-up a Consolidated Liberator of the RAF's Strategic Air Force, Eastern Air Command, before its participation in a daylight raid in November 1944 on the docks, railways and shipping at Rangoon in Burma. There were three squadrons equipped with these heavy bombers in India at the time. These were 150 Squadron based at Digri and equipped with Mark IIIs, Vs and VIs, and 355 and 356 Squadrons, both based at Salbani and equipped with Mark VIs. These Liberators could carry a maximum of 12,800lb of bombs.

Author's collection

(*Right*) The shadow of an RAF Liberator of the Strategic Air Force, Eastern Air Command, during a low-level attack on a road bridge between Pegu and Martaban, part of the Japanese supply line to Mandalay and the Arakan. Falling bombs can be seen in the photograph.

Author's collection

(*Below*) Bomb craters showing direct hits on the railway at Ye-U, about 85 miles north of Mandalay, attacked by Allied squadrons while ground troops were advancing towards the central plain in December 1944. This was one of the main supply lines for the Japanese forces.

Author's collection

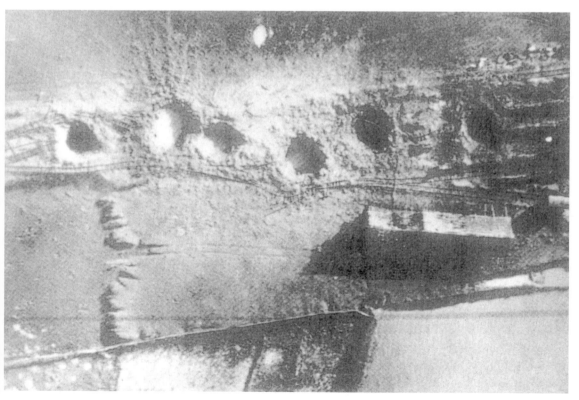

(*Above*) Lord Louis Mountbatten in 1944 reviewing photography personnel at RAF Dum-Dum, near Calcutta, before giving them a 'pep talk'.

Author's collection

(*Opposite top*) Spitfire PR XI serial PL776 at RAF Alipore in Bengal, where 681 Squadron was based from May 1944 to June 1945. This aircraft was flown from July 1944 to April 1945 by Wing Commander F.D. Proctor DFC, during part of the period when he commanded the squadron.

The late Wing Commander F.D. Proctor

(*Opposite bottom*) A Spitfire PR XI of 681 Squadron, with M. 'Bluey' George of the RAAF in the cockpit, possibly photographed at Chandina in India. George joined the squadron as a flight sergeant and was commissioned by early 1945. The cameras were F8s, used by the RAF in the 1930s for high-altitude photography. Most of these had been withdrawn after the introduction of the F52 camera, but several were purchased from the Indian Government for use over Burma.

The Medmenham Club

One of the five North American B-25C Mitchell bombers transferred to the RAF from the Military Aviation Arm of the Royal Netherlands Indies Army, probably serial number N5-143 when in Dutch service. These were converted to long-range photo-reconnaissance and placed on the strength of 681 Squadron. The photograph was taken in 1944 at Comilla in India.

F.W. Guy via G.J. Thomas

Corporal Alan Fox holding an F24 camera at RAF Dum-Dum in 1944. Although a ground photographer, he volunteered for aircrew duties in the photo-reconnaissance B-25C Mitchells and flew on seventy-five hazardous sorties over South-East Asia and the islands in the Bay of Bengal. He was awarded the DFM. After the war he eventually became one of Britain's most distinguished sociologists.

Alan Fox collection

Moulmein airfield, in the south of Burma near the mouth of the Salween river, photographed by an Allied reconnaissance aircraft.

Author's collection

(*Above*) RAF Beaufighters attacked a train on a line branching north-west off the main Rangoon–Mandalay line, from Pyinmana to Kokkogan. It caught fire immediately, emitting clouds of smoke which indicated that it was carrying oil for the Japanese forces.

Author's collection

(*Opposite top*) Hurricane Mk IV fighter-bombers, which could carry 500lb of bombs, were employed extensively in the Burma theatre of war. This Hurri-bomber was photographed in September 1944, showing two bombs falling from its wings during an attack on a bridge on the Tiddim road, already hit by an aircraft from the same squadron.

Author's collection

(*Opposite bottom*) The wagons of a goods trains being attacked by another Beaufighter after the locomotive had been brought to a halt and was emitting smoke and steam.

Author's collection

The 20mm cannon shells fired by an RAF Beaufighter against the oil pipeline between Rangoon and Myingyan (south of Mandalay) resulted in this huge spurt of blazing oil.

Author's collection

A farm cart trundling along a country road near Kyaukpadang (south-south-west of Mandalay) was spotted by RAF Beaufighters. Its load looked suspicious and one pilot attacked. Smoke rose in a huge black pillar from petrol burning on the road.

Author's collection

It was known that moored paddle-steamers on Burmese rivers, camouflaged with cut vegetation, were used by the Japanese as military headquarters. One of these houseboats was picked out and attacked by RAF Beaufighters which set it on fire with 20mm cannon shells.

Author's collection

An RAF Beaufighter attacking the locomotive of a goods train between Thazi and Pyawbwe, south of Mandalay, in January 1945. Clouds of steam are surrounding the locomotive after it has been hit by 20mm cannon shells.

Author's collection

(*Above*) Lieutenant-General Sir Oliver Leese (Commander-in-Chief of Allied Land Forces, South-East Asia, from 12 November 1944 to 6 July 1945) being driven in a jeep by Major-General Francis W. Festing (Commander of the 36th British Division from 16 November 1944 to 29 August 1945). Holding a rifle behind is a bodyguard, Corporal Joe Robinson of Swinton in Manchester. The jeep was approaching the village of Tonlon in North Burma in November 1944.
Author's collection

(*Opposite top*) After crossing the Chindwin in December 1944, troops of the Fourteenth Army advancing south-eastwards had to manhandle their armour over steep hills, scrubby jungle and chaungs (rivers). The troops in this photograph are fording a shallow stretch of the Nanson Chaung.

Author's collection

(*Opposite bottom*) Supply trucks crossing a pontoon bridge in the Chin Hills, along a road constructed from Imphal in India to Tiddim in Burma, where British and Indian troops were operating.

Author's collection

(*Above*) A supply convoy on the winding mountain road in the Chin Hills, between Imphal in India and Tiddim in Burma, hacked out to supply British and Indian troops in the forward area facing Japanese divisions.

Author's collection

(*Opposite*) Fusilier B. Thompson (left) of Ramsgate in Kent and Fusilier W. Robertson of Edinburgh, both of the 36th British Division's Royal Scots Fusiliers, manning a forward position approaching Mawle, near Pinwe, north of Mandalay, in November 1944. The Royal Scots Fusiliers and the East Lancs Regiment, together with British and Indian engineers and British and Chinese artillery, had advanced 75 miles from Hopin in fourteen days against Japanese defences in the jungles of Burma. This is a single photograph, although it appears to be two.

Author's collection

(*Above*) The 36th British Division had advanced southwards from Mogaung to Pinwe, about 120 miles north of Mandalay, by 30 November 1944. This photograph shows a battery of six mortars firing salvoes at Japanese positions near Pinwe railway station, on the main railway line leading down to Mandalay.

Author's collection

(*Opposite top*) A battery of the Royal Artillery firing a 24-pounder at Japanese positions during the battle for Pinwe in late November 1944.

Author's collection

(*Opposite bottom*) A battery commanded by Major G.T. Huckett of the 36th British Division firing 3.7-inch howitzers at Japanese positions in the hills near Pinwe in early December 1944.

Author's collection

(*Above*) Following a link-up with the 5th Indian Division, which had advanced eastwards from the Chindwin river, the 36th British Division fought its way south to within 12 miles of Ye-U, about 85 miles north of Mandalay, on 30 December 1944. This photograph shows troops of the 36th Division moving up to the front a few days later.

Author's collection

(*Opposite*) By Christmas Day 1944 armour of the Fourteenth Army had assembled at Pyingaing, between Kalewa and Shwebo (the latter about 30 miles north-west of Mandalay), and began to drive east to link up with other forces. This photograph shows Sherman and Lee-Grant tanks in January 1945, making their way along the dry river bed of the Bipadon Chaung. Japanese defences were quickly overcome.

Author's collection

Two men of the South Wales Borderers, Company Sergeant-Major Watkins and Private A. Lovell, both from Monmouthshire, patrolling in front of the Bahe Pagoda. Their regiment was part of the 36th British Division, in turn part of the Northern Combat Area Command. This had fought its way down the corridor of the Myitkyina–Mandalay railway, covering 150 miles in five months, before capturing the village of Bahe in central Burma.

Author's collection

This Bailey bridge on pontoons over the Chindwin river was 1,150 feet long and was completed by Indian sappers and miners on 10 December 1944 after only twenty-eight hours' work. It was the longest of its kind in the world.

Squadron Leader J.D. Braithwaite collection

CHAPTER SIX

Outwitting the Japanese

The march southwards of the two divisions and three brigades of IV Corps, under the command of Lieutenant-General Frank W. Messervy, was long and arduous. The route they had to follow was no more than a narrow and winding track with a poor surface. One of the main problems occurred when vehicles had to pass each other, one carrying supplies and the other returning empty for another load. The sappers had to work miracles to widen the track, especially at the points where it passed through hilly country. They also had the task of constructing airstrips where transport aircraft could land and from where tactical aircraft could support the troops. Some supplies came in by air and casualties were evacuated, despite the reduced capacity of the transport aircraft following the dispatch of three squadrons to China. These operations were partly achieved by diverting some of the Dakotas and Commandos from supplying the forces in the Arakan area.

Another intense worry concerned the vital need for secrecy, for the eventual thrust was intended to take place against lightly held Japanese positions on the eastern bank of the wide Irrawaddy near Pakokku. Special provision was made to deceive the enemy. A dummy headquarters for IV Corps was set up in Tamu, relaying false wireless messages to its fictional divisions in the Central Front. Misleading news broadcasts were also made, while the real IV Corps maintained strict wireless silence on its march southwards. These transmissions were picked up by the Japanese, convincing them that the entire IV Corps was still operating in the Shwebo Plain. They were aware that the 19th Indian Division of IV Corps was continuing to fight in the theatre, although did not know that on 19 December 1944 Slim had transferred it to XXXIII Corps, for operational reasons.

Formation signs on uniforms and vehicles of the IV Corps divisions heading for Pakokku were removed, while signs relating to the 11th East African Division were issued, although this division was in reserve at the time. There remained the possibility that Japanese reconnaissance aircraft might bring back photographs of this large-scale southern movement, but the air superiority achieved by the Allies was so absolute that any venturesome Japanese aircraft were shot down.

The most serious obstruction took place on 10 January 1945, when the leading units reached the village of Gangaw about 120 miles along the route of the march, while the main body of IV Corps was strung out behind them. This village was defended by Japanese in fortified positions, and it would have been imprudent to attack them in strength and perhaps disclose the true identity of the approaching divisions. The solution was found in an 'earthquake' attack by Allied air squadrons. Although not so intensive as similar attacks in the European theatre, this was nevertheless considerable. Four squadrons of B-25 Mitchells from the US 12th Bombardment Group swept over, with each aircraft unloading about 3,000lb of bombs on the enemy positions. These were followed by three tactical RAF squadrons, one of Thunderbolts and two of Hurricanes, making low-level strikes with bombs, cannon and rockets. The fighter-bombers then made feint attacks immediately ahead of the advancing troops, ensuring that the defenders kept their heads down. The attacking troops consisted solely of the Lushai Brigade, only lightly armed. They quickly cleared up all the remaining Japanese defenders, who were probably still stunned from the explosions. Soon after this success, Slim sent the Lushai Brigade to the rear for a well-earned rest, since it had been in action for most of the previous twelve months.

The advance then continued, with some troops taking to jungle paths to bypass and then encircle small contingents of Japanese defenders in their path. The next opposition occurred when the 114th Infantry Brigade, part of the 7th Indian Division, ran into strongly defended positions on high ground about 8 miles to the west of Pakokku. The first infantry attack was thrown back and it was not until 10 February, when tanks were brought in, that the Japanese were driven out.

Meanwhile the long track behind the attackers was being widened to permit the passage of more tanks as well as heavy vehicles bearing river craft. Sufficient supplies had to be brought to forward positions before the vital thrust could be made. A stretch of the Irrawaddy near Pakokku was being examined by ground reconnaissance patrols and from air photographs to identify the most suitable crossing places on both sides of the river. These crossings would be timed to coincide with other actions across the Irrawaddy in the Central Front. Continuing the deception tactics, fake maps were planted where they could be picked up by the Japanese, indicating that the objective was the recapture of the oilfields at Yenangyaung towards the south. These maps were also lent apparent authenticity by rumours deliberately circulated among the local population, including requests for the best means of reaching Yenangyaung.

This was not the only advance southwards, for the third Arakan campaign was taking place in the Mayu peninsula, forming another part of the co-ordinated Allied attacks on the various fronts in the Burma theatre. The northern region of the peninsula was still occupied by IV Corps, commanded by Lieutenant-General Sir Philip Christison. This had become a formidable force, having been built up to four divisions, plus a Commando brigade and a tank brigade. It was supported by tactical aircraft of the RAF's 224 Group, consisting of thirteen squadrons of Beaufighters, Hurricanes, Thunderbolts, Spitfires and Lightnings, under the command of Air Vice-Marshal the Earl of Bandon. There was also support from the sea by the Arakan Coastal Force commanded by Captain J. Ryland of the Royal Indian Navy. This consisted of three flotillas, each of about seven motor launches, and the depot ship HMS *Kedaw*.

XV Corps was opposed by part of the Japanese 28th Army, commanded by Lieutenant-General Sakurai Seizo and consisting of the 54th and 55th Divisions together with the 72nd Independent Mixed Brigade. In turn, these consisted of infantry regiments and battalions, plus an artillery unit and an engineer unit. However, the bulk of the 54th Division had been moved to the Irrawaddy delta, protecting the sea approaches to Rangoon, while only a single regiment of the 55th Division was stationed in the northern region of the Mayu peninsula. The Japanese forces remaining in this area could do little more than employ delaying tactics, although they always fought with their usual determination.

The offensive began on 12 December 1944 when the 82nd West African Division under Major-General G.McI.I.S. Bruce advanced towards Buthidaung on the east of the Mayu range, the scene of much fighting in the previous Arakan campaigns. This town was duly occupied three days later and a further advance began to the south. An assortment of about 600 river craft had been assembled at the little port of Maungdaw on the west coast. These small vessels were transported by road within the next five days through the tunnels of the Mayu range to carry supplies along the Kalapanzin, as the Mayu river was named in its upper reaches. Then the 81st West African Division, by then commanded by Major-General F.J. Loftus-Tottenham, advanced once more down the Kaladan Valley on the east. At the same time the 25th Indian Division, under the new command of Major-General G.N. Wood, struck down the narrow coast road on the west, fringed by mangrove swamps and tidal creeks known as 'chaungs'. The 26th Indian Division under Major-General C.E.N. Lomax and the 3rd Commando Brigade were meanwhile in reserve awaiting an amphibious operation to reoccupy Akyab Island, planned to take place within the next few weeks.

The two West African divisions made good progress and made a concerted attack on the Japanese communications centre of Myohaung, about 30 miles south-east of their starting points. This town fell to them on 25 December 1944 after a stiff fight, despite Japanese reinforcements which had been brought in from Akyab Island. The 25th Indian Division made equally good progress down the west coast, supplied from the sea, and on 26 December 1944 reached Foul Point on the southern tip of the Mayu peninsula.

It was then time for the amphibious operations against Akyab Island, carefully prepared with cruisers, destroyers, sloops and landing craft from the Royal Navy, but on 2 January 1945 an artillery officer flying in a light aircraft over the island saw local people making signs asking him to land. He did so and found that all the Japanese battalions had departed, to reinforce those fighting the West Africans in the Mayu peninsula. This was a welcome anti-climax and the island

Invasion craft approaching the island of Akyab on 3 January 1945. Lying off the west coast of Burma, Akyab had been under Japanese occupation since May 1942. The British troops on board the craft were supported by RAF and USAAF squadrons of Air Command, South-East Asia.
Author's collection

Troops beginning to wade ashore from landing craft at Akyab on 3 January 1945.

Author's collection

was rapidly occupied without conflict. An immediate start was made on restoring the major airfield, which had been damaged by Allied bombing and Japanese demolition. At last a swathe of Japanese-held territory in southern Burma came within easier range of the RAF and USAAF tactical squadrons, while their transport aircraft were provided with an all-weather staging post.

Christison then began the next part of his planned operations. The Japanese were in full retreat from the Arakan, heading southwards down the only road available for tanks and heavy vehicles, a few miles from the indented western coast. If this road could be cut, they would be trapped. The coast itself was a pestilential labyrinth of narrow chaungs and mangrove swamps, without landing beaches and almost entirely unmapped, but part of it had been secretly reconnoitred and marked by Combined Operations Pilotage Parties. The place selected for an invasion was the small peninsula of Myebon jutting southwards from the mainland about 30 miles south-east of Akyab.

On 12 January 1945 there was a preliminary bombardment of the area of Myebon village by the RIN sloops *Narbala* and *Jumna*, together with attacks by forty-eight B-25 Mitchells of the US 12th Bombardment Group. Then troops of the 3rd Commando Brigade, commanded by Brigadier Campbell R. Hardy, waded ashore from landing craft against light opposition, under cover of a smokescreen laid by the RAF. Thunderbolt and Hurricane fighter-bombers from the RAF's 224 Group made low-level attacks on enemy positions while Spitfires and Lightnings maintained fighter patrols above. The 74th Indian Brigade, part of the 26th Indian Division, arrived on the next day under the command of Brigadier J.E. Hirst. The invaders even managed to get some Sherman tanks and bulldozers ashore, after sappers had blasted rocks on the shore to provide a hard landing place. A counter-attack by a Japanese force, hastily scratched together, was repulsed and the whole peninsula was occupied by 17 January.

The next phase was another combined operation, embarking from the peninsula and landing on the coast beyond in order to push inland and occupy the village of Kangaw, about 8 miles east of Myebon. It was estimated that about 5,000 Japanese were still to the north of this village, withdrawing from the Arakan while being followed by troops of the 82nd West African Division.

This second seaborne operation took place on 22 January, under the cover of bombardment from the same sloops and the same air squadrons, but the Japanese were better prepared and immediately mounted a counter-attack against the bridgehead, accompanied by heavy artillery fire. The Commandos fought back and eventually occupied a hill position, repulsing attack after attack from Japanese at brigade strength. They then went over to the offensive and occupied Kangaw on 29 January. The Japanese were reinforced and made another ferocious attack which was eventually beaten off, leaving about 340 dead on the field. Meanwhile the 74th Indian Brigade pushed ahead from the Myebon peninsula and made contact with the leading elements of the 82nd West African Division moving south. Caught between two forces, the remaining Japanese at

Kangaw scattered eastwards, leaving behind a total of over a thousand dead, as well as many guns and vehicles, plus large quantities of equipment. According to Slim, this had been the critical operation of the whole Arakan campaign.

While these conflicts were taking place, Christison turned his attention to Ramree Island to the south of Akyab Island, defended by Japanese forces estimated to number about a thousand. The north-west tip of this island was invaded by a brigade of Lomax's 26th Indian Division on 21 January 1945. The assault was preceded by gunfire from the battleship HMS *Queen Elizabeth*, the cruiser HMS *Phoebe*, two destroyers and two sloops, together with bombardment from about eighty-five B-24 Liberators of the Strategic Air Force. Close support for the invading troops was provided by Thunderbolts and Mitchells of the RAF's 224 Group. There was little opposition from ground troops but a motor launch and a landing craft were sunk by mines. The beachhead was secured and another brigade from the same division landed on the following day.

Advances then began down the island, which was about 50 miles in length, against stiffening opposition. Japanese positions on the western seaboard were outflanked although the defenders fought with their usual stubbornness. Meanwhile Royal Marines landed on Cheduba Island to the south on 26 January and found that it was unoccupied by Japanese.

The Japanese on Ramree were forced to retreat eastwards to a region of mangrove swamps infested by crocodiles, and all effective resistance on the island had ended by mid-February. The survivors faced appalling conditions while hunted by their pursuers, but they refused to surrender. Some tried to escape over about 10 miles of sea to the mainland, in small craft or on improvised rafts made of bamboo poles plugged at both ends, but they were attacked by RN warships and bombed by the RAF. There appears to be no accurate record of the number of survivors.

The occupation of Ramree and Cheduba was of huge significance to Slim's strategy, for these islands provided bases for an eventual combined operation on the coast south of Rangoon. However, the next phase in his plans was the crossing of the Irrawaddy and the crushing of the Japanese armies in central Burma. Under operation 'Capital', the main assault was to be via the crossings by IV Corps in the region of Pakokku while the Japanese forces in Burma under the overall command of Lieutenant-General H. Kimura were being led to believe that this was merely a diversion for the main attacks over the river near Mandalay.

As part of this deception, the Fourteenth Army was maintaining pressure in the Shwebo Plain. The 19th Indian Division under Major-General T.W. Rees, by then part of XXXIII Corps, had reached the upper Irrawaddy at Thabeikkyin, about 65 miles north of Mandalay, on 9 January 1945. This was defended on both sides of the river but the division began to clear the west bank. Rees then managed to slip some patrols over the river. By 14 January he had established a bridgehead at Thabeikkyin and another about 20 miles to the south. The Japanese began ferocious attacks on these, but were repulsed with heavy losses. The 19th

(*Right*) Troops wading ashore from landing craft at Akyab on 3 January 1945. The Japanese had evacuated the island a few days before. RAF Spitfires landed on the island the day after these landings. They destroyed several Nakajima 'Oscar' fighter-bombers which attempted to strafe the British troops.

Author's collection

(*Below*) A tank of the 25th Indian Division, commanded by Major-General G.N. Wood, pursuing the Japanese withdrawing from the Myebon peninsula on the west coast of Burma, after the reoccupation of Akyab on 3 January 1945.

Author's collection

Division was strongly supported by the RAF, for Vincent had moved his fighters and fighter-bombers of 221 Group forward to the Shwebo Plain and these were able to respond almost immediately to requests from the ground forces. Rees was able to extend his bridgeheads and even go over to the offensive.

To the north of these actions, the 36th British Division under Major-General Frank W. Festing had pushed south in two columns, one of which was approaching Thabeikkyin. This division was still part of the Northern Combat Area Command under Lieutenant-General D.I. Sultan, whose Chinese divisions were also advancing south. Sultan had lost two of his earlier divisions, sent back to China as demanded by the Generalissimo, but the three remaining were positioned east of the 36th British Division and advancing in the face of Japanese opposition. There was also the Mars Brigade, which had been formed with mixed American and Chinese troops on 26 July 1944 and was now in action.

In the south-east of the Shwebo Plain, the 20th Indian Division under Major-General D.D. Gracey, also part of XXXIII Corps, had reached Myinmu on the Irrawaddy about 35 miles west of Mandalay. This occurred on 22 January 1945 and the troops were soon in combat with a party of Japanese trying to cross the river to the south bank. After a sharp conflict, most of the enemy troops were wiped out. Then the remaining Japanese troops formed ranks and marched in close order to the river and drowned themselves, to the amazement of the onlooking British and Indian troops. They had possibly run out of ammunition and could fight no longer. Gracey then sent reconnaissance patrols over the river at night, harassing the Japanese and keeping them on the alert.

These operations along the Irrawaddy convinced Kimura that the main thrust would be against Mandalay. He had over 200 miles of the river to defend and obviously could not station troops along its entire length. He disposed some of his forces at the most likely crossing points but kept strong reserves, including artillery and tanks, to deploy them wherever and whenever they were required. It soon became known to Slim that Kimura had withdrawn some of his regiments from the Pakokku area to assist in the defence of the Mandalay area.

Slim moved his headquarters to Monywa in the Shwebo Plain in early February 1945 and was joined by the headquarters of the RAF's 221 Group. This was a position from which he could collect intelligence from the various front lines and even visit them. He intended the major thrusts to be made almost simultaneously, but left his divisional commanders in the front lines to select the best points along their sectors of the Irrawaddy.

The first of these thrusts took place on the night of 12/13 February when the 20th Indian Division began crossing as silently as possible in the vicinity of Myinmu. Two landing places had been chosen, based on air reconnaissance which indicated that the Japanese were present in no great strength on the southern banks. The positions were between the Japanese 31st and 33rd Divisions, part of the 15th Army commanded by Lieutenant-General S. Katamura. The Irrawaddy was about 1,500 yards wide in this stretch and the

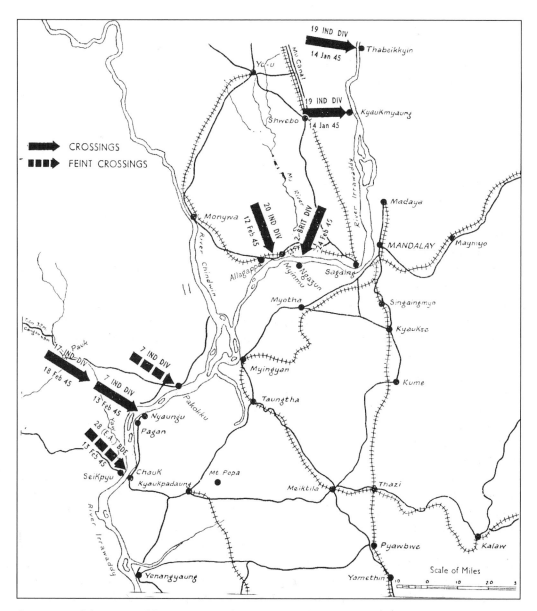

Crossings of the Irrawaddy, January–February 1945. This map is copied from the *Report to the Combined Chiefs of Staff by the Supreme Commander South-East Asia 1943–1945*, published by HMSO in 1951.

attackers experienced difficulties from wind, currents, sandbanks and faulty outboard motors, with some landing craft being swept further downstream. Nevertheless the landings were made against slight initial opposition, and the troops were able to start digging in.

More troops and supplies came over during the following nights. The Japanese did not counter-attack in any strength until 15 February, by which time the two bridgeheads had joined up to become 6 miles wide and 2 miles deep. RAF Hurricane fighter-bombers of 221 Group were remarkably successful in knocking out thirteen Japanese tanks with their rockets and cannon, and all the attacks were repulsed. The Japanese fell back by 27 February, leaving over 700 dead on the field, probably plus many more who could not be counted.

The front around Pakokku in the south presented more difficulties. The current of the Irrawaddy was much stronger below its confluence with the Chindwin. There were also more sandbanks, so that the crossings had to be oblique, making them about 2,000 yards in length. These crossings by divisions of IV Corps began a day after those at Myinmu, on the dark night of 13/14 February. Three crossing places had been chosen, with two of them as feints to confuse the enemy. There were no initial or accompanying bombardments from the air, thus indicating that the landings were no more than small diversionary tactics. On the opposite bank were some units of the Japanese 15th and 28th Armies, strung out and thinly held over a wide area, and the somewhat ineffective 2nd Division of their Indian National Army.

The 7th Indian Division commanded by Major-General G.C. Evans was given the task of making two of these initial crossings and forming bridgeheads. The main crossing was in the centre, about 8 miles south-west of Pakokku, and headed for the town of Nyaungu on the east bank, a few miles from the ancient capital of Pagan. On its left flank a feint crossing by the 7th took place from Pakokku itself, headed for the east bank. On its right flank the other feint crossing was made by the independent 28th East African Brigade commanded by Brigadier W.A. Dimoline, headed for Chauk on the east bank. Its purpose was to continue with the deception that the ultimate objective was the oil centre of Yenangyaung to the south.

The main crossing went well in its initial phase, with a company of the 2nd South Lancashire Regiment reaching the east bank and scrambling up cliffs to dig in. Some of the other crossings went awry, with boats beaching on sandbanks or being swept downstream when outboard motors failed, then coming under fire. However, the situation was gradually rectified, with more troops pouring across on the next day, covered by artillery fire and air bombardment.

The Japanese reacted violently to the 28th East African Brigade, believing this to form the main thrust. Fortunately there was no opposition at Pagan, for the Japanese garrison had departed for the Mandalay area and left its defence to troops of their Indian National Army, who promptly surrendered and laid down their arms. Thus the splendid orange-red pagodas of this ancient capital, numbering over a thousand, were spared the destruction of a modern bombardment. Some of the Japanese at nearby Nyaungu retreated into a network of defensive caves. The entrances were blown in and sealed, leaving them to die of starvation or commit suicide.

The next phase was a crossing by the 48th and 63rd Brigades of the 17th Indian Division commanded by Major-General D.T. Cowan, together with the 255th Indian Tank Brigade commanded by Brigadier C.E. Pert. These had been waiting in the rear of the other troops, unknown to the Japanese, but they now came forward and between 18 and 21 February were ferried over the Irrawaddy. The 99th Brigade of the 17th Indian Division had not taken part in the long advance to Pakokku but had been left far behind at Palel, about 25 miles south of Imphal, in preparation for an airborne operation against Meiktila when the other two divisions neared that crucial objective. Slim's deception plans were working satisfactorily.

The thrust towards Meiktila began immediately after these three brigades had assembled on the east bank. Both the 48th and 63rd Brigades had been fully mechanised and they advanced rapidly with the 255th Indian Tank Brigade. They split into two prongs, meeting little opposition, and joined up again at Taungtha on 24 February. Then they headed for the airfield at Thabutkhon, about 10 miles north-west of Meiktila, and reached it two days later after opposition from snipers and small suicide squads. The airfield was rapidly cleared and the next phase of Slim's plan went into operation, for the 99th Brigade of the 17th Indian Division began flying in, while fuel was also brought in for the tank brigade.

The advance continued but a strong road block was encountered outside Meiktila. This was bypassed by the infantry who attacked it from the rear while the tanks came in from the front. The Japanese were completely routed and the area of Meiktila became encircled. However, the garrison was larger than expected, almost 3,800 men, and a stiff fight lay ahead.

Meanwhile another threat against the Japanese in the Mandalay area began on the night of 24/25 February. The 2nd British Division commanded by Major-General C.C. Nicholson, part of XXXIII Corps, had reached the Irrawaddy about 10 miles east of the 20th Indian Division's bridgehead at Myinmu. It had gathered sufficient boats and equipment to begin an operation against the village of Magazun on the opposite bank. It was a clear moonlit night and the boats came under heavy fire, holing and sinking some of them. There was some confusion when some men were marooned on an island in midstream, but more troops came over and a bridgehead was formed on the opposite bank. The Japanese did not mount their usual attack, since at this time Kimura was regrouping his forces along this stretch of the Irrawaddy for a major assault. He did not seem to appreciate the acute danger in his rear at Meiktila.

Nor did Major-General Kayusa, the commander of the Meiktila area, realise the threat to his town until too late. His forces were widely spread in various

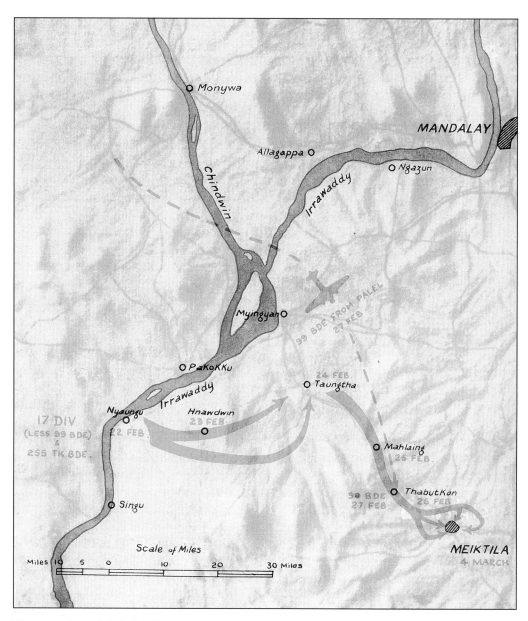

The assault on Meiktila, February–March 1945. This map is copied from the *Report to the Combined Chiefs of Staff by the Supreme Commander South-East Asia 1943–1945*, published by HMSO in 1951.

airfields, supply dumps and communication lines. Nevertheless he acted with the utmost speed and gathered about 3,200 men together, including some from hospitals who were still able to stand, and issued them with arms and ammunition. There was protection for the town from lakes and irrigation canals to the south and west, but the attackers came in with tanks, artillery and infantry from other directions. Many of the encounters took place at close quarters in streets, buildings and basements, with the Japanese fighting with their usual determination and ferocity. They were not completely wiped out until 3 March, when almost 900 of their bodies were counted in one area alone. Some of the survivors committed suicide.

In the course of these actions, Slim heard some very unwelcome news. The Generalissimo had demanded that the Chinese–American forces in Burma should cease their advances on the Northern Front and be flown to China, in order to participate in a forthcoming offensive against the Japanese. This was extremely worrying, partly since the US transport squadrons were essential for the campaign of the Fourteenth Army. Mountbatten's protests to Chungking were fruitless, but as a compromise the US and British Chiefs of Staff agreed that major transfers to China should be delayed until 1 June or until Rangoon was recaptured, whichever was the sooner.

The unexpected occupation of Meiktila by the 17th Indian Division was extremely alarming for Kimura, who suddenly realised the grave threat in the rear of his forces in the Mandalay area, cutting off their supply line. He ordered Lieutenant-General M. Honda, the commander of the 33rd Japanese Army, to recapture the town. Regiments, battalions, artillery and a few tanks were pulled away from the area of Pakokku, the Arakan and even some that were trying to contain the bridgeheads over the Irrawaddy near Mandalay. These troops amounted to two divisions but were not a cohesive force. Their separate columns heading for Meiktila came under ruthless attack by the RAF and some were ambushed en route by detachments of Cowan's 17th Indian Division operating from Meiktila.

The Japanese were determined to regain the main airfield, about 3 miles west of the town centre, which was already being used by transport aircraft of the RAF. On 15 March these brought in from Palel in India a brigade of the 5th Indian Division, by then commanded by Major-General E.C.R. Mansergh. Soon afterwards, aircraft landing at the airfield came under artillery fire, for some Japanese had arrived in the hills to the north. Fierce fighting followed and it was not until 29 March that the fly-in of the other brigades of the 5th Indian Division was completed and the Japanese were entirely eliminated. The battle for Meiktila and its later defence cost IV Corps 835 killed and about 3,250 wounded or missing, but the Japanese losses were far heavier. Even then, mopping-up of Japanese contingents in the Meiktila area was carried out.

During the capture and defence of Meiktila, divisions of XXXIII Corps in the area of Mandalay began major advances from their bridgeheads over the

Irrawaddy. The first of these was the 19th Indian Division commanded by Major-General Rees. One of the brigades broke out of its bridgehead north of Mandalay on 26 February and was rapidly followed by the other two. These swept south against remnants of the 15th Japanese Army, which had almost disintegrated after fruitless attacks against the bridgeheads, and reached the north-east of Mandalay on 8 March. Two brigades went into the attack but two days earlier the third had been sent east to the vital town of Maymyo, which dominated the main road and rail supply line to the Japanese facing the Chinese–American forces of the Northern Combat Area Command.

Defence of the outskirts of Mandalay was confined to small groups of Japanese, but the areas of its central hill and Fort Dufferin proved much stronger. The hill, about 800 feet in height, was covered with temples and numerous gun emplacements had been prepared. The fighting began on 9 March and continued for three days and nights, hand-to-hand and of extreme ferocity. The attackers, mostly Gurkhas and British, gradually cleared the emplacements, with the Japanese fighting to the last man. The few remaining retreated into cellars, where they were incinerated when petrol drums were rolled down inside and then set alight by tracer bullets.

Fort Dufferin was a huge rectangular enclosure, defended by walls 23 feet in height, 30 feet thick at the base tapering to 12 feet at the top, with a surrounding moat. Artillery fire with 5.5-inch shells failed to blast holes in these. B-25 Mitchells tried to breach them on 15 March with 2,000lb bombs dropped from 6,000ft, but these missed the walls and instead destroyed buildings inside. Three RAF Thunderbolt squadrons tried on the next day with 500lb bombs directed from low level at the inside walls, again without success. Eventually, the Thunderbolts attacked from the outside, over the moat, and some partial gaps were made. A 'forlorn hope' attempt to storm through these would have been very costly, but on the morning of 20 March a group of Anglo–Burmese came out with white flags. The Japanese had crept out through drains during the night and abandoned the fort, leaving European and Anglo–Burmese civilian prisoners behind, as well as booby traps and large quantities of stores.

The prize of Mandalay had fallen to the 19th Indian Division. Moreover the brigade that headed for Maymyo had cleared this town of the enemy and then, apart from a battalion left as a garrison, it had marched to rejoin the other brigades. In ten weeks of fighting since reaching the Irrawaddy, this division had counted 6,000 Japanese dead in combat.

Meanwhile, the other two divisions of XXXIII Corps broke out from their bridgeheads over the Irrawaddy near Mandalay. The 2nd British Division under Major-General C.C. Nicholson was nearer to this city and had expanded to the east and west. Its advance along the bank continued eastwards, against small parties of Japanese, until it reached the town of Ava, where the long bridge over the Irrawaddy had been blown during the retreat of 1942 but never repaired. The resistance was much stiffer in this town but the Japanese were cleared out by 17 March.

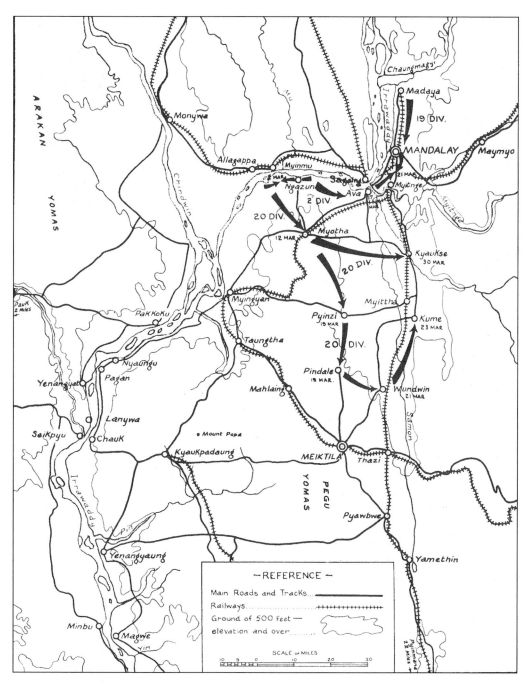

Advances by Fourteenth Army around Mandalay in March 1945. This map is copied from the *Report to the Combined Chiefs of Staff by the Supreme Commander South-East Asia 1943–1945*, published by HMSO in 1951.

Further to the west the 20th Indian Division under Major-General D.D. Gracey had not only enlarged its bridgehead but repelled all attacks so effectively that the Japanese were exhausted. Headed by an armoured column, the three brigades broke out to the south-east on 8 March and four days later reached Myotha, a junction on the Meiktila–Mandalay railway line. The Japanese resisted stubbornly but were overcome. From there, one brigade circled further east and on 21 March reached Wundwin on the Rangoon–Mandalay railway line. This was the administrative centre for the Japanese 18th Division, and once the defenders had been killed many supplies were captured. The brigade then struck north, destroying tanks, guns and transport, and even capturing a hospital full of sick and wounded patients. Meanwhile the other two brigades struck due east from Myotha towards Kyaukse on the same railway line. This was strongly defended and it was not until 30 March that it fell and enormous quantities of supplies were captured.

Official casualty figures for the three divisions of XXXIII Corps during these breakouts from bridgeheads were given as 1,472 killed, 4,933 wounded and 120 missing, apart from those incapacitated by sickness. Although serious numbers, they represented only a fraction of those inflicted on the Japanese, whose armies in central Burma had almost disintegrated during the battles.

In all these operations the ground troops had received close support from the RAF. This dominated the skies in its tactical and strategic work, having expanded to a total of seventy-one squadrons equipped with modern aircraft. There had been a change in the top command, for Air Chief Marshal Sir Richard Peirse had been relieved of duty on 27 November 1944. His replacement was to have been Air Chief Marshal Sir Trafford Leigh-Mallory, who had commanded the Allied Expeditionary Air Force during the invasion of Normandy, but his aircraft had disappeared on 14 November when bringing him out to take up his appointment. The wreckage of the crashed aircraft was not found until seven months later, in the French Alps. Pierse's deputy, Air Marshal Sir Guy Garrod, took over command until the arrival on 24 February 1945 of Air Chief Marshal Sir Keith Park, who had achieved fame in the Battle of Britain and in Malta.

On 1 April the 36th British Division under Major-General Festing was returned to the Fourteenth Army after its service with the Northern Combat Area Command. Relations with the Americans and Chinese had been excellent but operations had declined after many Japanese had been withdrawn from the area to reinforce their armies in central Burma. The Chinese–American forces were being sent to China while NCAC was reduced to about 500 armed tribesmen under American officers, guarding the eastern stretch of the Ledo Road which had been completed on 27 January 1945. Slim welcomed the return of his division and ordered Festing to head for Mandalay and support the 19th Indian Division, which was still busy mopping up Japanese forces scattered around the city.

RAF ground mechanics servicing the engine of a de Havilland Mosquito in India. Mosquitos operated with great effect against Japanese strongpoints and supply lines, but their wooden airframes could deteriorate in tropical conditions. Only a single photo-reconnaissance squadron served over Burma in May 1943 but four squadrons in the light bomber role had been added by March 1945.

Author's collection

A mosaic of Mergui airfield, near the coast in the south of the Kra Isthmus, facing the Indian Ocean, photographed by an Allied reconnaissance aircraft.

Author's collection

Troops of the Fourteenth Army fighting in the Lushai Hills, east of Chittagong in India, were partly supplied by local river craft called 'khastis', manned by Nepalese soldiers of the Indian Pioneer Corps. This photograph taken in February 1945 shows Pioneers struggling with the rapids on the Karnaphuli river.

Author's collection

Air Vice-Marshal S.F. Vincent, Air Officer Commanding 221 Group RAF from 17 February 1944 to 12 June 1945.
Author's collection

Lieutenant-General M. Honda, Commander of the Japanese 33rd Army.
Author's collection

Major-General G.C. Evans, Commander of the 7th Indian Division from 29 December 1944 to 7 February 1946. As a Brigadier, he had commanded the 9th Indian Infantry Brigade from 14 to 25 February 1944, and then the 123rd Indian Infantry Brigade from 25 February to 21 July 1944.

Author's collection

Major-General C.G.G. Nicholson, Commander of the 2nd British Division from 5 July 1944 to 2 April 1946. He had previously commanded the 21st Indian Division from 17 April to 5 July 1944.

Author's collection

While the long-range heavy bombers of the RAF and the USAAF in the Eastern Air Command concentrated mainly on targets in Burma, those in the 14th USAAF based in China under the command of Brigadier-General C.L. Chennault made attacks elsewhere. This B-24 Liberator was photographed turning for home after bombing railroad repair shops at Vinh in French Indo-China, near the Gulf of Tonkin about 180 miles south of Hanoi. Clouds of smoke from bomb explosions indicate direct hits.

Author's collection

Bombs dropped in March 1945 by RAF Liberator VIs of 231 Group, Air Command, South-East Asia, destroyed a railway bridge at Kalawthut, 22 miles south of Moulmein in Burma, as shown in this photograph taken from 500 feet. The southern part of this railway from Bangkok to Rangoon was built by British prisoners-of-war under appalling conditions of forced labour and starvation.

Author's collection

(*Above*) Supplies being dropped in December 1944 from a C-47 Dakota of the RAF to British and West African troops of the 81st West African Division, XV Corps. These had advanced more than 50 miles in forty days through dense jungle in the Pi Chaung and Kaladan Valleys on the Arakan Front in Burma, to occupy the village of Mowdok.

Author's collection

(*Opposite top*) Tanks of XV Corps advancing with guns firing against Japanese positions on the Arakan Front in March 1945.

Author's collection

(*Opposite bottom*) Units of the Royal Navy, the Royal Indian Navy, the Royal Canadian Navy and the South African Navy participated in the landings of 3 March 1945 on Akyab Island. Destroyers, minesweepers, sloops and motor launches supported the ground troops.

Author's collection

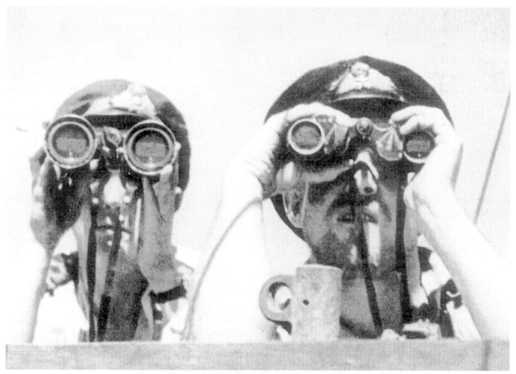

A heavy and concentrated attack was made in January 1945 by B-24 Liberators of RAF and USAAF squadrons in the Strategic Air Force, Eastern Air Command, against the airfields of Mingaladon and Zayatkwin near Rangoon. There was low cloud but the targets could be seen through gaps and there were no enemy fighters. This photograph shows bombs falling from two RAF Liberators.

Author's collection

The Ledo Road was opened on 27 January 1945, having taken American engineers over two years to build. It was 483 miles long and started from the railhead of Ledo in India, before winding up the passes of the Patkai Range and the upper Chindwin river, to connect with the town of Wanting in an area of the pre-war Burma Road which had not been occupied by the Japanese. The first supply column to set off for Kunming in China, a total of 1,040 miles, is shown here.

Author's collection

217

A unit of Kachin hill tribesmen formed part of the 36th British Division, Northern Combat Area Command, when fighting southwards from north Burma. This Kachin patrol was photographed in February 1945 moving through the burning village of Tonnges, near the town of Tigyaing, which had harboured Japanese military police.

Author's collection

Outwitting the Japanese

Lieutenant-General Sir William J. Slim (born 1891), outside his headquarters at Monywa in central Burma in early 1945. Among themselves, his troops of the Fourteenth Army referred to him as 'Uncle Bill'.

Author's collection

Soldiers of the Fourteenth Army, flown in by air, firing mortars at Japanese positions among the gold and white pagodas in Meiktila. The attack on this vital town was not expected by the Japanese, and its fall on 3 March 1945 cut off the escape route of their troops in Mandalay, 80 miles to the north.

Author's collection

(*Above*) Infantrymen of the Punjab Rifles, Fourteenth Army, advancing from Meiktila under cover of a Sherman tank, after the capture of the town on 3 March 1945.

Author's collection

(*Opposite*) Troops of the Fourteenth Army advancing behind an armoured vehicle through the undergrowth from the town of Meiktila. The town, 80 miles south of Mandalay, was cleared of the enemy on 3 March 1945 after a lightning strike across the Irrawaddy. It was the centre of land communications in Burma. After airfields in the area were cleared, strong airborne forces were brought in and much fierce fighting followed.

Author's collection

(*Above*) Gurkhas and other troops of the 19th Indian 'Dagger' Division, Fourteenth Army, crossing the Irrawaddy with laden mules to one of their bridgeheads north of Mandalay in February 1945.

Author's collection

(*Opposite top*) A Bren carrier crashing through the devastated outskirts of the little village of Ywathitgyi in the Irrawaddy basin on the road towards Mandalay, in the face of fierce Japanese opposition.

Author's collection

(*Opposite bottom*) After liberating the ancient city of Pagan at the end of February 1945, British forces of the Fourteenth Army advanced north-east towards Mandalay. This night photograph shows British gunners firing a 7.2-inch howitzer against Japanese positions defending the important city.

Author's collection

British troops of the 19th Indian 'Dagger' Division, Fourteenth Army, filtering through the outskirts of Mandalay in early March 1945.

Author's collection

Troops of the 2nd British Division, Fourteenth Army, advancing along the south bank of the Irrawaddy towards Mandalay in early March 1945. They had driven a wedge between the Japanese forces in the area, with the aid of artillery fire, and the ground was littered with enemy dead.

Author's collection

On 19 March 1945 RAF Liberator VIs of 231 Group, Air Command, South-East Asia, made sorties of over 17 hours from India to attack railway sidings at Na Nien, 8 miles west of Chumphaun in the Gulf of Siam. They went in at low level, setting trains and oil tanks on fire. People were seen waving to them as they crossed over the Kra Isthmus.

Author's collection

Some of the damage from the RAF's attack on Na Nien, showing wrecked coaches and trucks, torn railway lines and gutted administration buildings.

Author's collection

Gunners of the 19th Indian 'Dagger' Division firing point-blank at Fort Dufferin in Mandalay, the last stronghold of the Japanese in the city. It was protected by walls a mile square, a rampart 23 feet high and a wide moat. It fell on 20 March 1945 after a siege lasting twelve days.

Author's collection

Private A. Brain from Banbury in Oxfordshire resting on his rifle after the capture of Fort Dufferin in central Mandalay on 20 March 1945. This was the last remaining stronghold of the Japanese in the city, which had been entered twelve days earlier by British and Indian troops in a strong armoured column of the 19th Indian 'Dagger' Division, part of the Fourteenth Army.

Author's collection

CHAPTER SEVEN

Complete Destruction

The time had arrived to launch a combined operation to recapture Rangoon, the next objective in the final elimination of the Japanese forces in Burma. It was imperative to reach the capital before the summer monsoon restricted movement. There was also the need to complete the operation before the American transport squadrons were withdrawn to China by the scheduled deadline of 1 June. The outcome was a race against these eventualities as well as against enemy contingents which were still numerous. Although the Japanese were disorganised and bereft of almost all armour and artillery, they would still fight fanatically and might yet be able to regroup.

Slim decided to mount his assault with a two-pronged attack from the north by ground troops. One prong would consist of IV Corps' 5th and 17th Indian Divisions, together with the 255th Tank Brigade, which would advance along the single road leading down the railway axis from Meiktila to Rangoon. The other prong would consist of XXXIII Corps' 2nd British Division and 20th Indian Division, together with the 268th Indian Brigade, based in the Mandalay area. Slim originally considered dispatching these down the road along the railway corridor from Mandalay, but they would be held up by too many blown bridges. Thus they were ordered to cross far over to the west, join up with the 7th Indian Division of IV Corps, and then follow the roads down the banks of the Irrawaddy. The arrival of either of these two forces near Rangoon would coincide with an amphibious invasion to the south of the capital, codenamed 'Dracula', which would be coupled with a descent by paratroops.

The regrouping of the divisions lasted several days. Most of the men had been fighting for several months but morale was high after their succession of victories and they were also eager to finish the campaign. When those of XXXIII Corps reached their new positions to advance down the Irrawaddy, the 2nd British Division became heavily involved in combat with Japanese in entrenched positions on Mount Popa, an extinct volcano rising 5,000 feet above the plain. These positions were not cleared until 20 April and the division did not take part in the thrust southwards but was then held in reserve.

Meanwhile the 7th Indian Division, which had been transferred to XXXIII Corps, made good progress down the Irrawaddy against slight opposition and captured the oil wells of Yenangyaung on 22 April. The Japanese seem to have

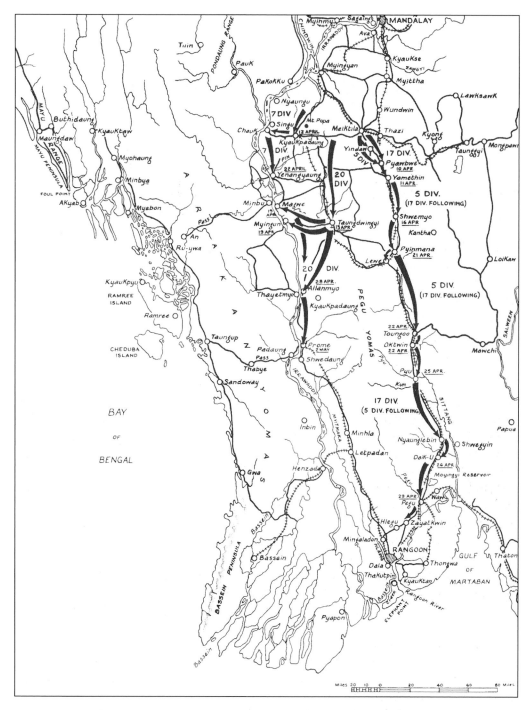

Fourteenth Army's advance towards Rangoon, April–May 1945. This map is copied from the
Report to the Combined Chiefs of Staff by the Supreme Commander South-East Asia 1943–1945,
published by HMSO in 1951.

been taken by surprise, for they lost heavily and the rest scattered. On the left flank of the 7th, the 20th Indian Division struck southwards and then cut eastwards to occupy Magwe on 19 April. It then thrust southwards down the east bank of the Irrawaddy and reached Prome on 2 May, over 100 miles from Rangoon, where it had to wait for supplies being brought by road and river.

The advance towards Rangoon of IV Corps, consisting of the 5th and 17th Indian Divisions and the 255th Tank Brigade, made good progress down the railway axis after leaving Meiktila on 31 March. These forces had the advantage of being supplied from the air. The road ahead was about 300 miles long but, with the use of tanks and tactical air support, the divisions took turns in smashing Japanese defences, leaving many enemy dead while changing the lead for the next section of road. On 29 April the 17th reached Pegu, about 45 miles from the outskirts of Rangoon, to find it strongly defended. Kimura had been ordered to protect Rangoon and had gathered three battalions prepared to fight to the death. There was also an unexpected deluge of pre-monsoon rain so that the Pegu river, normally fordable, went into flood while forward airstrips for the RAF were put out of action. The Japanese blew the bridges over the river and fought desperately before they were eliminated. Then the 17th had to wait for engineers to repair the blown bridges before tanks and transport could cross. The official casualty figures for IV Corps during the march from Meiktila to Rangoon were 460 dead or missing and 1,706 wounded. The troops counted 6,742 Japanese dead and 273 prisoners. They also destroyed or captured tanks, guns and lorries.

D-Day for the amphibious landing south of Rangoon was 2 May. Six convoys had left Akyab Island and Ramree Island from 27 April onwards, carrying men of the 26th Indian Division from XV Corps. They were escorted by a cruiser, four aircraft carriers and four destroyers. More air cover was provided by six tactical squadrons from the RAF's 224 Group and eight squadrons of B-25 Mitchells from the US 12th Bombardment Group. In addition, the battleship HMS *Queen Elizabeth* and the French battleship *Richelieu*, together with cruisers, aircraft carriers and destroyers, had sailed from Ceylon to prevent any interference by the Japanese Navy. On 30 April these destroyers sank nine of eleven Japanese transports in the Gulf of Martaban, carrying a thousand Japanese troops from Rangoon towards Moulmein. Unknown to the British, Kimura had ordered the capital to be evacuated.

On the day before D-Day, a battalion of Gurkhas from the 50th Indian Parachute Brigade was dropped by Dakotas over Elephant Point on the far south of Rangoon river. This was the only occasion when paratroops were employed in the Burma campaign. The Gurkhas quickly overcame slight defence and advanced towards Rangoon. On the following day, the crews of the naval vessels succeeded in putting the troops of the 26th Division safely ashore, after bombarding all known Japanese positions. These troops sloshed northwards in torrential rain, expecting conflict ahead.

During the afternoon a Mosquito VI of the RAF's 110 Squadron was flown on

The Japanese evacuated Rangoon at the end of April 1945 but the Allies were not sure of this until an RAF Mosquito pilot read messages on the roof of the gaol: 'BRITISH HERE JAPS GONE. These were painted partly to avoid the possibility of a bombing attack.

Squadron Leader J.D. Braithwaite collection

The PoWs in Rangoon gaol added 'EXTRACT DIGIT' to their roof notices, an expression which was unmistakably that of British servicemen. Parachutes descending with supplies can be seen in the top right of this photograph. A Mosquito pilot landed on nearby Mingaladon airfield and walked to meet the senior officer in the gaol, an RAAF wing commander.

Squadron Leader J.D. Braithwaite collection

reconnaissance over Rangoon by the commanding officer, Wing Commander A.E. Saunders. He and his navigator saw huge letters painted on the roofs of the main gaol, reading BRITISH HERE JAPS GONE EXTRACT DIGIT. This was so unmistakably RAF 'speak' that they landed at nearby Mingaladon airfield. The Mosquito was damaged on the bombed runway but the two men walked unharmed to the gaol, where they met the senior officer, Wing Commander L.V. Hudson of the RAAF, and discovered that 1,400 prisoners were there but no Japanese. Then they went to the docks, commandeered a sampan and sailed to meet the troops and relay the news. Thus the RAF, already held in high regard by the ground forces, was the first to arrive in Rangoon. The ground troops marched triumphantly into the city, where they were welcomed by thousands of cheering inhabitants.

Germany surrendered unconditionally on 5 May, and V-E Day was celebrated ecstatically three days later in Britain. The men in Burma shared less in this elation. Some of the British had had no home leave for over four years. They were winning their battles and the Japanese were in retreat throughout the Pacific, but it seemed that they would be finally conquered only when their homeland had been invaded and fought over at the cost of immense casualties. Meanwhile, the Allied forces in Burma had plenty of work on hand. The Japanese between Meiktila and Rangoon, numbering about 20,000 men, had been split into three sections by the two-pronged advance of XXXIII Corps and IV Corps down the Irrawaddy valley and the railway corridor. In addition, there were about 50,000 more elsewhere in Burma, mostly part of the 33rd Army east of the Sittang river and in its delta region.

The most intensive fighting at this stage took place in the Irrawaddy valley, where about 10,000 men of the 54th and 55th Divisions, part of the Japanese 28th Army, were isolated. Some of them were situated west of the river and needed to break out eastwards. The first attempt began on 11 May about 30 miles north of Allanmyo on the Irrawaddy and lasted for five days. Many of the enemy were destroyed by the 7th Indian Division, which also captured seventy-five lorries.

Those Japanese who evaded the 7th Division then moved south to the village of Kama, about 20 miles north of Prome, where the main body of Japanese was crossing the Irrawaddy. The 7th Division and the 268th Brigade engaged this force and fierce fighting followed. Most of the enemy west of the river were destroyed while two cordons were positioned around the bridgehead to encircle those on the east bank. From 21 May onwards the Japanese made repeated efforts to break through the inner cordon and reach the jungle-clad hills named the Pegu Yomas. The 54th Division was split into two columns, one commanded by Major-General T. Koba and the other by Lieutenant-General D. Miyazaki. Further south, elements of the 55th Division and 28th Army Headquarters with miscellaneous units also pushed eastwards towards the Pegu Yomas, as did a naval force and an independent mixed brigade.

These suffered casualties but others managed to slip through. The outer cordon was thickened with more troops but some Japanese passed through in small parties, losing all their transport and almost all their guns. It was the monsoon period and RAF aircraft were hampered by clouds. The Allies counted 1,400 Japanese bodies, but others lay undiscovered or were wounded. Those who survived faced the perils of the jungle, starvation and disease. They needed to reach the Sittang river and link up with their 33rd Army.

A unit of the clandestine Force 136, operating behind Japanese lines and commanded by an experienced Jedburgh named Major Thomas A. Carew, had made contact with the leader of the Burma National Army, Aung San, who had prudently decided to change sides. With the prior agreement of Admiral Mountbatten, he and a staff officer were given safe conduct. They passed over the Irrawaddy north of Prome on 15 May and were flown to Slim's headquarters in Meiktila. Dressed as a major-general in a uniform similar to that of the Japanese Army, Aung San offered in fluent English to fight the Japanese provided he was given immunity from prosecution as a traitor. Slim found him not unlikeable, although he placed little value on his army as a regular fighting force. By prior arrangement with Mountbatten, he agreed on condition that the Burmese obeyed the orders of British commanders. They were given the new title of Patriot Burmese Forces.

On 28 May major changes began in the command structure. The new Twelfth Army was formed under Lieutenant-General Sir Montague Stopford to command all operations in Burma, while the Fourteenth Army was reformed in India under the command of Lieutenant-General Sir Miles Dempsey, who had commanded the Second Army in Europe. Sir William Slim was promoted to General and appointed to succeed Lieutenant-General Sir Oliver Leese as commander of the Allied Land Forces.

The Fourteenth Army in India then had under its control the new XXXIV Corps, commanded by Lieutenant-General Ouvrey L. Roberts and consisting of the 5th, 23rd and 25th Divisions. It also controlled a Commando brigade, a parachute brigade, armoured and artillery regiments, and a Royal Marine regiment. All these began training to invade the west coast of Malaya under operation 'Zipper', scheduled to take place at the beginning of the dry season in September 1945, accompanied by a huge fleet from the Royal Navy and covered by the equivalent of twenty RAF squadrons.

Other units were withdrawn to India to follow this first wave for the invasion. The new Twelfth Army in Burma then consisted partly of IV Corps, under the temporary command of Lieutenant-General F.I.S. Tucker while Lieutenant-General Sir Frank Messervy was on leave. In turn, IV Corps consisted of the 17th Indian Division under Major-General D.T. Cowan and the 19th Indian Division under Lieutenant-General T.W. Rees, together with the 268th Indian Infantry Brigade under Brigadier G.M. Dyer and the 255th Indian Tank Brigade under Brigadier C.E. Pert. There were also five battalions of Aung San's Patriot Burmese Forces, acting mainly as guerrillas. In addition to IV Corps, the Twelfth Army also controlled other forces, mostly on the Irrawaddy Front. These

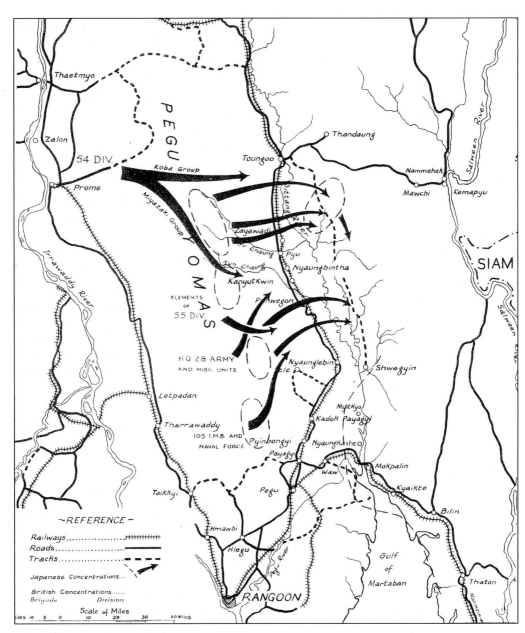

The Japanese retreat towards Siam, as on 19 July 1945. This map is copied from the *Report to the Combined Chiefs of Staff by the Supreme Commander South-East Asia 1943–1945*, published by HMSO in 1951.

were the 7th Indian Division under Major-General G.C. Evans, the 20th Indian Division under Major-General D.D. Gracey, the 82nd West African Division under Major-General H.C. Stockwell and the 22nd East African Brigade under Brigadier R.F. Johnstone.

Sir Montague Stopford expected the remnants of the Japanese 28th Army to break out of the Pegu Yomas, where the more able-bodied survivors were foraging in the jungle while others were dying of wounds or sickness. To meet this anticipated 'Battle of the Breakout', he withdrew forces from the Irrawaddy Front to reinforce those of his IV Corps strung out in a line to the east of these hills, with concentrations at the more likely escape tracks.

A battle began on the night of 3/4 July, not with this breakout but with about 10,000 men of the Japanese 33rd Army in the south-east area of the Sittang river, who struck north-west in the direction of the communications centre of Waw. This was an effort to draw troops away from the defensive line awaiting their 28th Army. Stopford had advance notice of the attack from captured documents, and had placed the 7th Indian Division in positions ready to repel it. The ground was completely waterlogged, up to waist depth in places, but with some villages and a railway embankment on higher ground. The Japanese attacked with their usual ferocity but were repelled again and again, with help from the RAF when the weather was clear enough. They held off and resorted to shelling, but the 7th retreated out of range while carrying their wounded. The Japanese made one more attack but were repelled once again and their efforts petered out.

The breakout from the Pegu Yomas began on 20 July, with parties of up to about 600 Japanese descending from the hills and then trying to fight their way across the road. These parties did not arrive simultaneously and kept using the same routes. Troops of IV Corps dealt with each, in combination with the RAF making their usual strafing and bombing attacks. The Japanese could not dig in the waterlogged ground but some sought refuge in villages. Their survivors split into smaller parties and tried to reach the Sittang under cover of darkness. Those who escaped ambush, partly from the Patriot Burmese Forces, came under more fire when trying to cross the river on improvised rafts. Over 600 of their bodies were counted floating down the river at one of the crossing points. The last to make the attempt were about 1,200 Naval Guards on 31 July, but all save three were slaughtered.

It was all over by 4 August, by which date some 5,000 bodies had been counted by IV Corps. The Japanese estimated that about 12,000 men of their 28th Army were killed or missing from approximately 17,500 who had made this attempt. IV Corps took the remarkable total of 740 prisoners, indicating that at last Japanese morale was beginning to crack. The Corps lost only ninety-five killed, thus beating the enemy at the rate over a hundred to one. This was the last battle in Burma, although the Japanese were still being harried and killed by Burmese guerrillas raised and armed by Force 136.

By this time the Japanese homeland was in a parlous condition. The country's air force and navy had been so depleted that only suicide missions were possible,

A distant photograph of the atom bomb dropped on Nagasaki on 9 August 1945. The Japanese sued for peace after this second atom bomb and agreed to surrender unconditionally five days later.
Author's collection

although its army still consisted of about two million fully equipped men prepared to fight to the death. The economy was in a shambles, since production depended mainly on imports of raw materials and the country was completely blockaded. Cities and towns were being systematically destroyed by air bombardment while ports were being shelled by Allied warships. Foodstuffs had become so inadequate that starvation was looming. Many military leaders realised that surrender was inevitable.

President Harry Truman, Winston Churchill and Marshal Stalin met at Potsdam on 17 July to discuss their requirements for the surrender of Japan, in the knowledge that the new atom bomb had been developed. They agreed that the surrender must be unconditional and that the country should be occupied. Chiang Kai-shek agreed to the declaration when he read it, but Stalin did not sign since the official policy of Russia towards the Japanese war was still that of neutrality. The declaration was signed by the others on 26 July and passed to Japan on the following day. It warned that failure to accept the terms would result in the complete destruction of the Japanese armed forces and the devastation of their country.

The Japanese dithered, hoping to extract some concessions before acceptance. In the early morning of 6 August three Boeing B-29 Superfortresses approached the city of Hiroshima, overlooking the Inland Sea on the south coast of Japan's Honshu Island. These had taken off from the US air base on Tinian Island, one of the Mariana Islands in the Pacific, and two were in the role of observers. The

Life returning to Hiroshima in January 1947. This view is of the main street with the telephone exchange still standing, although the interior of the building was gutted by the heatwave of the atom bomb dropped on 6 August 1945.

Jim Muncie collection

other, flown by Colonel Paul Tibbetts and bearing the name of his mother, *Enola Gay*, dropped a 20-kiloton atom bomb named *Little Boy* over the centre of the city at 0815 hours. The Japanese later gave their casualty figures as 76,150 killed and 51,048 injured from a population of 343,000, and stated that almost all the buildings in the city had been destroyed or badly damaged.

Even then, Japanese General Headquarters did not capitulate. The raid was obviously extremely severe but at first seemed less destructive than a low-level raid made earlier by the US XXI Bomber Command over Tokyo on the night of 9/10 March, when a colossal firestorm had resulted in the deaths of 84,020 people and injuries to over 40,000 others. Some Japanese experts were aware that the Allies, as well as Germany, had been researching atomic power but they did not know that an atom bomb had been developed. At the time accurate reports were arriving from Hiroshima, an atom bomb named *Fat Man* was dropped at 1130 hours on 9 August from a B-29 named *Bock's Car* over the town of Nagasaki on the west coast of Japan's Kyushu Island. This missed the exact centre of the town but 23,753 people were killed and 43,020 injured.

Emperor Hirohito accepted unconditional surrender on the following day, in the knowledge that his country faced a new and terrible weapon. Most Japanese servicemen immediately accepted his order of surrender but some small units in Burma were cut off from communication and continued to fight. These were harried by ground forces and bombed by the RAF for several more days before the campaign ended.

The official battle casualty figures for the British and Commonwealth land forces in Burma from December 1941 to August 1945 were eventually listed as 14,326 killed, 44,731 wounded and 14,552 missing. Most of those recorded as missing were lost in the 1942 retreat and many of them became PoWs, perhaps not to survive. Equivalent figures from the Japanese do not seem to be available but must have been many times higher than these.

V-J Day was celebrated in Britain on 14 August but the occasion was muted by comparison with that of V-E Day. The war in Burma seemed remote, far fewer British servicemen were in the Far East, and people were busy trying to rebuild their lives in conditions of extreme economic difficulties, acute shortages of consumer goods, strict rationing of food and heavy taxation.

On 2 September Japan signed an instrument of surrender in the presence of General Douglas MacArthur, appointed as Supreme Commander of the Allied Powers, on board the battleship USS *Missouri* in Tokyo Bay. For Britain the Second World War had thus lasted for six years less one day. The efforts of the forces in Burma moved to restoring civilian rule within South-East Asia, and above all, to rescuing the Allied PoWs who had somehow survived the sadistic brutality of their Japanese captors. Operation 'Zipper' took place on 9 September on the beaches of Port Swettenham in western Malaya, but it was merely a tactical exercise witnessed by crowds of cheering Malayans.

Admiral Lord Louis Mountbatten insisted that a surrender ceremony should take place in Singapore, attended by all high commanders of the Japanese land, sea and air forces which had fought in this region. On 12 September General Sir William Slim sat on the left of Mountbatten, within a line of the principal Allied commanders. The Japanese had to give up their swords, and Slim felt no soldierly empathy with them during the ceremony when they affixed their seals to the surrender document. A Union Jack flew over the building. It was the same one that had accompanied the flag of truce when Singapore surrendered on 15 February 1942. It had been hidden by prisoners in Singapore jail as a symbol of hope for those who survived.

A Sherman tank advancing south down the open central plain of Burma after the fall of Mandalay on 20 March 1945

Author's collection

A Lee-Grant tank of the Fourteenth Army driving south with infantry through the mid-Burma plains towards Rangoon after the successful capture of Mandalay on 20 March 1945.

Author's collection

Men of the RAF Regiment on patrol in search of Japanese stragglers as they retreated south down the central plain from Mandalay in late March 1945.

Author's collection

Living conditions for personnel of the RAF's 681 (PR) Squadron in April 1945 when on detachment at Monywa, close to the Chindwin river in the central plain of Burma, about 40 miles west-north-west of Mandalay. The squadron was equipped with Spitfire PR XIs and its main base was RAF Alipore, near Calcutta.

Wing Commander G.J. Craig collection

On 18 April 1945 RAF Liberator VIs of 231 Group, Air Command, South-East Asia, attacked canals west of Bangkok after railway bridges in the area had been destroyed. Wrecked lock gates and sunken shipping can be seen in this photograph.

Author's collection

The city of Prome, a railhead along the Irrawaddy basin about 120 miles north-north-west of Rangoon, was captured on 2 May 1945 by the 20th Indian Division commanded by Major-General D.D. Gracey. This armoured column came under fire from both sides of the road, but the Japanese were swiftly eliminated.

Author's collection

Two strange vessels, flying the White Ensign, approaching Rangoon river on 1 May 1945. They were built by the Inland Water Transport Service for the Fourteenth Army. Made of wood, they had lightly armoured bridges, steamed at 12 knots, and were armed with a Bofors gun, two Oerlikon guns and two Browning machine-guns. General William Slim named them HMS *Pamela* after Admiral Mountbatten's younger daughter and HMS *Una* after his own daughter, without permission from the Admiralty. They saw much active service on the rivers of Burma as well as on the approaches to Rangoon.

Author's collection

This RAF reconnaissance photograph taken from low-level over Rangoon, before it was reoccupied on 3 May 1945, showed Japanese gun positions to be heavily cratered and abandoned.

Author's collection

A mosaic of Victoria Point airfield, on the most southerly tip of Burma in the Kra Isthmus. This was intended to be an important base for the RAF in Operation 'Zipper', the Allied invasion of Malaya.

Author's collection

Infantry and tanks moving north to Rangoon towards blazing buildings, against fire from the Japanese. A Gurkha battalion, brought in by Dakotas, landed by parachute on Elephant Point on 1 May 1945. The 26th Indian Division linked up with these paratroops after landing the following day on both sides of the Rangoon river, carried by vessels of the Royal Navy.

Author's collection

In June 1945 the Japanese forces were retreating eastwards across the Pegu Yomas towards Siam, pursued by the Twelfth Army. This Japanese sniper was brought in by a British infantryman to one of the villages near the city of Pegu, the ancient capital of Burma, about 50 miles to the north of the modern capital of Rangoon. He appears to have been stripped of his uniform and then bound and blindfolded, for security reasons.

Author's collection

The Japanese tanker *Toho Maru* of 10,000 tons in flames before sinking in the Gulf of Siam on 15 June 1945. She was spotted sailing north under escort by a Sunderland based near Rangoon, and twelve RAF Liberators of 231 Group, Air Command, South-East Asia, made a long sortie from India to deliver an attack. The weather was extremely difficult but nine Liberators found the vessel and she was hit by four bombs.

Author's collection

Troops of the Royal Gurhwal Rifles searching Japanese prisoners in Kuala Lumpur, Malaya, after V-J Day on 15 August 1945.

Author's collection

A Japanese officer in front of a Tachikawa Ki-36 army co-operation aircraft at RAF Mingaladon, near Rangoon, photographed by the author after V-J Day. Such Japanese prisoners were treated humanely by the British, in contrast with the brutalities inflicted on Allied prisoners, but they had to obey all orders 'at the double'.

Author's collection

A C-47 Dakota of the RAF's 52 Squadron being loaded at Meiktila airfield in central Burma, photographed by the author soon after V-J Day.

Author's collection

A Japanese mechanic working on an engine at RAF Mingaladon, photographed by the author after V-J Day. Such men worked hard and efficiently for the Allies after they had been ordered to surrender by Emperor Hirohito.

Author's collection

Bibliography

Brown, Arthur. *The Jedburghs: A Short History*. Unpublished, 1995.

Brown, David. *Warship Losses of World War Two*. London: Arms and Armour, 1990.

Donald, David. *American Warplanes of World War II*. London: Aerospace Publishing, 1995.

Fox, Alan. *A Very Late Development*. Coventry: University of Warwick, 1990.

Halley, James J. *The Squadrons of the Royal Air Force & Commonwealth 1918–1988*. Tonbridge: Air-Britain, 1988.

Howard, Michael. *British Intelligence in the Second World War*, vol. 5. London: HMSO, 1990.

Kirby, S. Woodburn. *The War Against Japan*, 5 vols. London: HMSO, 1957–69.

Loosmore, Glyn. *A Postscript to Arthur Brown's 'The Jedburghs'*. Unpublished, 1997.

Mikesh, Robert C. & Shorzoe, Abe. *Japanese Aircraft 1910–1941*. London: Putnam, 1990.

Mountbatten, Vice-Admiral the Earl of Burma. *Report to the Combined Chiefs of Staff*. London: HMSO, 1951.

Owen, Lieutenant-Colonel Frank. *The Campaign in Burma*. London: HMSO, 1946.

Probert, Air Commodore. *The Forgotten Air Force*. London: Brassey's, 1995.

Rawlings, John D.R. *Coastal, Support and Special Squadrons of the RAF and their Aircraft*. London: Jane's, 1982.

Richards, Denis & Saunders, Hillary St G. *Royal Air Force 1939–45. Vol. 2 The Fight Avails*. London: HMSO, 1954.

Roskill, S.W. *The War at Sea 1939–1945*. London: HMSO, vol. II, 1956; vol. III, pt 2, 1961.

Saunders, Hillary St G. *Royal Air Force 1939–45. Vol. 3 The Fight is Won*. London: HMSO, 1954.

Shores, Christopher and Cull, Brian with Izawa, Yasuho. *Bloody Shambles, Volume One*. London: Grub Street, 1992.

Slim, Field-Marshal Sir William. *Defeat into Victory*. London: Cassell, 1956.

Taylor, John W.R. *Combat Aircraft of the World*. London: George Rainbird, 1969.

Terraine, John. *Business in Great Waters*. London: Leo Cooper, 1989.

Thetford, Owen. *Aircraft of the Royal Air Force since 1918*. London: Putnam, 1988.

Index

Index